Other Titles by this Author

On the Other Hand: The Little Anthology of Big questions

Just Around the Bend: Más o Menos

Stepping Out of Time

Umbra, Penumbra & Me (a compilation)

The Doubt Factor

Children's Picture Books

The Frightened Little Flower Bud   Ages 4-99

Hat   Ages 6-99

Darkness holds the unknown, which can only
be revealed to us when we venture into it.

Before going any further, I'd like to point out that for the fluidity of this book, I use the pronoun we a great deal. This is how I see us; we're One. Yes, it's not always 100% appropriate to use the proverbial we, but for the purposes of this book its meaning is general.

LOUDER

Than

a

Whisper

Renée Paule

RPG Publishing

Louder than a Whisper: Clearer than a Bell

By Renée Paule

Edited by G R Hewitt

Copyright © 2015 Renée Paule

Published in France by RPG Publishing 2015

Cover design and illustrations by Renée Paule

Written in British English

ISBN: 978-2-9546811-8-4

Thank You

Godfrey for believing in me
and for all your help and support.

Mike

Susan

Hazel

.

No jargon!

Humanity
Each and every one of us as a 'whole'.

One
All that is, was or ever will be.

Ignorant
To ignore.

Intelligence
Independent and radical thinking.

Society
The world we've created for ourselves to live in,
with all its complex mechanisms.

Belief
A personal preference.

Hope
Waiting for a future event that may never arrive.

Fear
Dreading a future event.

Spiritual
Thinking outside the box and searching inside
ourselves for higher meaning.

For your convenience there are blank pages
for notes at the back of this book.

Table of Contents

Introduction

We can't see the truth about our world with closed minds.

Threads about a transformational journey through life (pilgrimages, paths, quests, purpose, etc.) are woven through music, poetry, symbols, paintings, films, documentaries and all literature; I just couldn't see the connections for a long time. They're in fantasy, games, hobbies, metaphors; they're in myths, theme parks, theatres, sports and legends too. There's so much information out there whether metaphorical or not; it's 'louder than a whisper; clearer than a bell', which is how this book got its title. We can't see it until we're ready to. We can't see it until we question our way of life and are willing to change it; until the way we live becomes more absurd than the idea that a legend may be trying to tell us something important. When we do see it, the absurdity of the way we live our lives becomes manifest and loses its appeal. This book isn't about those connections; it would take thousands of pages to write a book like that and involve a great deal of research which would be counter-productive - adding dubious knowledge rather than removing it. This book is about my journey, my quest, my change of mind and my determination to question everything - to destroy the assumptions that I once accepted as my reality, regardless of where it leads.

~~~

It was many decades ago that I struggled to write my first book - my autobiography. Struggling, because I was trying to write what didn't need to be written (my story of pain) instead of what did (my story of recovery); I was swimming upstream instead of down. It seems incredible that I'm now writing my third book and I've had a lot of time to think about why these books are coming out as they are - they're reflections of my ongoing journey and therefore, also semi-autobiographical.

I don't plan the chapters in any of my books but rather, I allow them to be written as a stream of consciousness. What didn't need to be written about was my life story and what did was how I learnt to 'let it go' - not allowing myself to be controlled by things from the past that can't be located, by us at least. What I'm really writing about is my psychological journey from helplessness, confusion and self-pity to inner strength - a journey of negation and a determination to find what's always been missing from my life; my purpose - a purpose - something to make waking up each morning feel worthwhile rather than mundane and repetitive. When I get stuck I sit in front of my computer and hold various questions in mind that are answered through my fingers onto a screen or, I move away from my desk and do something entirely different until what I'm going to write about becomes clear - it never takes very long. What's guiding me? I know that whatever it is, it's far greater than 'me'.

I used the term "brutally honest" in the blurb for On The Other Hand. One reviewer wrote that the book is "fiercely honest" and when I thought about that I questioned (as is my wont) what is it to be 'brutally' or 'fiercely' honest anyway? We're fractured to such an extent that we have levels of honesty and dishonesty which strikes me as rather ridiculous; either something's honest or it isn't; anything else comes from confusion and division. If 'brutal' honesty hits hard then it must have come face-to-face with brutal dishonesty in order to have that impact. Honest was what I needed to be in order to free my mind and it's by no means an easy trip. To see our reflection in the world outside can be a terrifying experience - far more so than the physical reflection we see when looking into a mirror. However, to see truth and the new - as veils of dishonesty are removed - is a priceless experience that can't be equalled and everyone can see these; we only have to question the undeniable pernicious chaos in our world. Many who question the reality of this world and philosophise about it are labelled 'insane' but regardless of whatever label anyone wishes to tag me with, my messages are written with love. For me to be told that I'm 'nuts' by others is one thing and it doesn't bother me at all, but when I initially began to question my own take on reality, it was another matter altogether.

If this book is about anything, then it's about changing weakness and fear into strength through a process of observation and self-examination; it's about turning the known world up-side-down and it's about walking blindfolded, without fear, along a gossamer thread knowing it can take the strain. It's clear to me now that it was my state-of-mind that prevented me from seeing what I'd known all along; here … now … this is it. So much is revealed to us when we're willing to examine our thoughts, actions and intentions - all of them. With this realisation I felt the almost 'evangelical' need to share it and much to my surprise I discovered just how difficult it is, if not impossible, to spread this message. What is it about Humanity that causes it to reject good news and treat it more like a repellent? When we're prepared to look at the world with new eyes from a wider perspective (non-subjective) it becomes a far more beautiful place to live in.

When covering so many simple topics that have become complicated by society certain repetition of thought is necessary and unavoidable. I do however, endeavour to keep this to a minimum. For this reason I may re-visit some points in more than one chapter; this is unavoidable and very much a part of the process of unlearning - some of our conditioning is harder to remove. If I repeat anything to you then I'm also repeating it to myself. It's not enough to ask the question 'Who am I' just once, as though it were a magic curative. It's part of a process that we need to be fully absorbed in rather than a hobby. We learnt what we know by rigid rules and strict repetition and we have to unlearn it in the same way with a new pilot at the helm - ourselves. When we reduce complexity to simplicity, we arrive at our point of origin, in this world at least.

Sensation, Desire & Relevant Reflections

We need so little, but desire so much.

Whilst walking past my local bakery I was stopped in my tracks by a tantalising smell. I was unable to make out if it was sweet or savoury but felt odd sensations that resembled 'cravings'. Regardless, the event was full of flavours, urges, feelings of pleasure and the irresistible 'come and get me' invitation that at one time would've had me walking through the door in an instant, carrying out further 'investigation'. It was while I was lost in these pleasant evocations that it occurred to me what a wonderful and interesting thing had happened - it was all from sensory memory. How is it, I wondered, that I've vastly different aromatic experiences when passing a fishmonger's shop - evoking less appealing memories. It was at that moment I decided to write about the abstract human trait that we call, desire.

Desire is a 'loaded' word generally associated with having sexual, gastronomical, financial or religious overtones:

- Sexual - to be desirable to or by another.
- Gastronomical - to desire food; for pleasure (excess?). Desire is not a word we use to describe the needs of people who are starving - food is essential.

- Financial - to bring us security; to eliminate personal lack of anything we want in this world for the duration of our lifetimes - but not beyond. Need is an entirely different thing; clothing, food and shelter.
- Religious - to bring us the greatest and most elusive prize of all; Heaven - if we manage to conquer our desires for anything other than God - but not until we die.

Little wonder our focus is on the first three of these; they're attainable within our lifetime. We've heard the word 'desire' or seen images being used in the above contexts more than any other - through subliminal messages and a great deal of early (often religious) conditioning. I told a few friends that I'm writing a chapter called 'Desire' (original chapter title) and asked what their initial reaction was to that word. To one it meant an expensive new car and to others it was an exciting new partner, improved personal appearance, happiness or an increase in wealth - things we're conditioned to set our sights on. Interestingly, the desire for answers to fundamental questions about the 'meaning of life' were not mentioned. Are we so lost in ourselves that these questions have become undesirable? One person did say they desire 'world peace' but hadn't thought about what that means or how it might be attained; 'world peace' has no more meaning to most people than any other throwaway cliché. In order to understand what desire is we first need to erase our conditioning through a process of enquiry - then look at it afresh. Without questioning the disorder in the world, we can't expect to create order.

~~~

'Want' can be interpreted as 'must have'. We always want more; such as money, a bigger house, car, television or better 'quality' gadgets and when - or if - we get them, we're not satisfied once the novelty wears off. Sometimes we can't fulfil our desires and in particular those we're encouraged to strive for. This leaves us with the feeling that there's a great void in our lives; for example, when we can't find 'romance', good friends or when we desire to be popular, have a 'top job' or at the very least, to be valued. Those of us who do have 'enough' material things are no happier than those who don't; we all have drawers full of discarded past desires. This comes about because the 'sensation' of desire is far more thrilling than the fulfilment of it and more importantly, it breaks the monotony of our limited daily lives.

Desire and temptation are closely connected and one can't exist without the other. In order to desire something, we must be able to be tempted by it. In the same manner, in order for temptation to exist, it must know desire. It's for these reasons that advertising is so powerful. Advertising companies have a great deal of experience and know exactly how to appeal to our senses - we provide them with the information. They also know that our desire for these sensory experiences override our need to be kind to ourselves or each other - they know that we prefer to say 'Yes' to any 'pleasure call' and they know us better than we know ourselves. I can't remember how many times I've bought packets of biscuits or cakes after having been tempted by the packaging and, on opening them, being disappointed by the stark difference between the image on the packet, and the contents. We know this to be the case yet still buy these goods and accept the disappointments as 'one of those things'. In time, we don't expect the contents to match the image; we accept the anomaly when we should be outraged by it and demand a refund. Just how far will we allow this situation to progress? Apathy leads to an insidious undervaluing of ourselves that lowers our expectations until one day, we'll likely be unperturbed if the packet is empty.

There's a tendency to desire what isn't good for us rather than what is and I'd suggest that this can be put down to a lack of self-worth - we both know and deny these things. As children we loved to put our hands into 'lucky dips' for the surprise, not because it was worth having, but because of the anticipation and excitement of it all - for the thrill. We loved playing 'pass the parcel', 'musical chairs' and participating in 'sports day' events, but they resulted in disappointment for all but the winner - who was sometimes disappointed too. We learn early on to cope with and accept setbacks that result in us feeling inadequate; we're not!

~~~

Advertisers tempt us into buying products we wouldn't want or need, by making them 'desirable' or 'fashionable'; for example, novelty party foods, ice dispensers on our fridge doors and new 'specialist' blister-plasters that heal self-inflicted wounds from wearing the fashionable shoes - allowing us to keep wearing them. In some commercial sectors 'demand' precedes production; sales of products and pre-orders are guaranteed well in advance. Because of demand the markets are saturated with colourful, shiny and attractive goods for us to desire and as quickly as we buy them, we discard them - rather like children who open a longed-for present at Christmas time or on their birthday and never touch it again. Who are the people who produce and advertise these things for us? We are! Humanity is its own villain, victim and hero.

There's an underlying sense of something lacking in our lives - a pernicious discontentment; it's a black hole that can never be filled no matter how much we stuff into it. Little wonder we easily become addicted to smoking, alcohol, sex, snacks, shopping, gossip, television, laziness or excessive exercise. When we're 'hurt', offended, depressed or feeling unworthy we want to suppress those feelings - to desire something 'uplifting' in their place, and after the initial lift has dissipated, nothing has changed - we're right back where we started and feeling just as empty, and perhaps a little guilty. Activities such as fulfilling an 'I need a drink' thought, exhausting ourselves with exercise, hibernating under our duvets or eating the contents of the fridge, provide only the coldest of comforts; they help us to cope with the surface of our woes rather than the root causes of them. Humanity is self-punishing, self-destructive and - with equal yet unused force - self-reflecting and self-healing.

How is it that we're caught in the loop of desire and disappointment? The problem is that we're reaching 'out' instead of 'in'; when we reach out, we place our trust in the hands of others that appear to be answering our 'call'. We feel 'low', see something that pleases our senses and as we need a 'lift' we react in a way that brings a superficial gratification, even though we know the 'hit' is instant and will leave us feeling dissatisfied after the event - the so called 'anti-climax'. I'd suggest that we tend to suffer with 'Now Syndrome' and that we're always looking for the next 'hit'. The actual timeless Now is never sad, lonely or depressing - these feelings require access to the past.

Despite remembering our painful past and looking towards our uncertain future, on a deeper level we always have and always will live in the 'Now' - it's impossible to be anywhere or 'anywhen' else. As discussed in 'Time', 'Time is an illusion obscuring the Now' and it's this illusion that leaves us groping for what we can get in the aberrational physical Now, even if it's a re-vamped version of something old - we see it as 'new'. We're in the Now when we're crying, angry, depressed, can't stand another moment without him, or her. The Now is when we self-punish because we see 'no way out' of a particular situation we've wrapped ourselves in.

The Now is when we find no immediate resolution to our woes and seek consolation from the 'decadence' we convince ourselves to eat, 'retail therapy', or the alcohol we recklessly consume - though these consolations are more punishing than they are anything else. We 'enjoy', yet at the same time, hate ourselves for succumbing to these comforting temptations and pastimes - a hate we justify because of our 'woeful' circumstances.

~~~

Desire is so much more than just 'wanting' things. There's something about a wrapped glittering package, prettied with ribbons and a label with our name on it. We love new things and we love surprises so these packages - as assembled under a Christmas tree for example - hold great appeal to our senses; the surprise adds a sensational element that excites us more than the gift itself. Some small children prefer the wrapping paper to the gift; it could be because they're unimpressed with the present or that they love the crackling sound of the paper and feel of the silky ribbons. Have you ever felt the disappointment of having no further gifts to open on Christmas day (if any at all) or seen a child searching under the tree in anticipation of finding another present with their name on it? These gifts appeal to our selfish side that claims 'They're mine'; try taking a toy from a young child or preventing them taking a toy from another - the result is a tantrum. Once opened, a gift can be cherished, admired or be a bitter disappointment, but none of these feelings can compare to the elevated sensations and concentrated delight we feel as we carry out the process of discovering what's inside. The gift stimulates multiple sensations that we enjoy feeling for reasons we don't give a second thought to - the adventurous expectation of what's inside. We love and can't live without sensations and in the case of gifts, the whole process of receiving them is over too soon.

We'd experience the same sensations and expectations even if a beautifully wrapped present contained no gift inside, provided we were unaware of that fact. We live in a multi-sense 'reality' so it's understandable that we seek to experience and re-experience these sensations in full. We love to repeat anything that brings pleasure, like a child shouting 'Again! Again!' to be thrown up in the air and safely caught in the arms of his father; unless we're exceedingly disciplined we say the same words to ourselves when we're grown up, to a packet of biscuits for example, until they're all gone. There are the five senses that tell us this world is 'real' - physical senses - but there are many more sensations that we like to experience such as excitement, elation, curiosity, pain, violence, misery and fear to name just a few; we have many more spiritual/abstract senses.

~~~

We harm ourselves when we watch the news, horror films or try to hold on to things that aren't good for us, like bad relationships and painful memories. We resist good advice and hold onto a perpetual 'not good enough' feeling - carried over from our pasts and re-lived in various forms many times every day. Why do we do it? I'd suggest it's easier to 'go with the flow' of society than it is to resist it - even if it's painful and disturbing. You may argue that we don't 'like' these things, but then it would be necessary to think about why we agree to suffer them, and put up such a huge resistance to doing without them. As I said in the introduction, 'We claim not to like violence, yet accept it as entertainment'.

Just as we feel the misery of others, such as on television, we can feel their excitement and happiness too; we love to see pleasure on the faces of others. For example, we love to see the faces of those who've achieved their goals, such as winners of races and competitions, or those who've succeeded to climb high peaks or overcome seemingly impossible difficulties from a position of hopeless weakness to one of towering strength. These are our heroes or role models and this is one of the reasons we accept the authority/celebrity status of others; we feel they've overcome difficulties to get to their positions and therefore, we hold them in high esteem - they've 'succeeded' where perhaps, we've failed. It's impossible not to be caught up in the energy of these moments or to react emotionally; we're attracted to - and repelled by - each other's energy fields like magnets. When we don't feel powerful, we enjoy bathing in the reflected glory of others - in effect, we're living our lives by proxy. It's a spiritual/abstract desire that we seek to fulfil through others, rather than ourselves.

The more I focus my attention on this subject, the more I see how incredible a human being is. Incredible in the sense of us being a wonderful piece of bio-engineering, but more in the sense of our crass foolishness and immaturity. One of the most bizarre traits we have is the desire to be desirable - to attract a mate. Advertisers go to great lengths to encourage us to be attractive to others with perfumes, fabrics, skimpy clothing, makeup, alluring images of men or women, encouragement to 'behave badly' and much more; in doing so, they tell us that we'll be (and are) undesirable if we don't use their products. There are no shortages of places we can go to fluff up our feathers in order to compete with the 'competition', and no shortage of 'hopefuls' trying to attract our attention.

We tend to be more and more outrageous in our desire to keep up with - or exceed - the expectations of our ever-changing disordered society, but grace, humility and wisdom are left far behind us in this race to 'fit in'. Disorder can only lead to further disorder. The most undignified display of attention seeking I've ever seen was at a railway station when a member of a teenage 'hen party' of half-naked girls held up a stick with a sex toy on it and asked the ticket collector if Mr **** needed a ticket; 'in what way will these impressionable girls become more outrageous' is a worrying question and I doubt very much that it will lead to their eventual happiness. It's highly unlikely that the group member with the sex toy 'tool' would dare to behave in this way outside the group - she'd feel far too vulnerable, at risk and afraid. Acting in this way will never make up for what's missing in our hearts, hopes or deeper desires; we're more than adequate without the assistance of commerce and it's 'highly recommended' degradation of ourselves. Under the façade and bravery of our outward behaviour and appearances - outrageous or otherwise - we know that there's so much more to us.

The suppression of our desires is an invitation for them to rise again at a later date - they can't be eradicated. Desire is innate and in particular the desire we suppress the most - the desire to know what our lives are really about; in its place we accept the desires of the commercial world that encloses us. It's natural, that when we suppress our true desires they must express themselves in a negative way; suppression holds us back and when that energy builds up inside us we must one day let it out. It's for this reason that our world is full of anger, depression, war and other negativity; we work in opposition to what we know is true and what we really want - this is how 'regret' is born. No matter how much we suppress our hearts' desires they will crop up again and again until we recognise them and we'll continue to suffer the painful consequences of our ignorance. Trying to ignore a desire is like pushing an inflatable ball into water - the more pressure that's used to keep it down, the more furiously it will one day rise up.

~~~

Desire is a human trait that can never be satisfied - the very meaning of the word denies fulfilment. By its nature, desire demands a gratification that we seek to experience again and again. We enjoy the sensations of getting what we want, because it feels like we've gained some sort of power over our lives by working hard for something or manifesting it - we believe we're in control. But in 'reality' we're not getting what we want because we don't know what we want; hence, we readily accept distractions that bring momentary pleasure. We're always getting what other people want for us and what we receive has become so limited that we believe 'version II' of a game, film, gadget or new relationship is something entirely 'new' and desirable; we choose to ignore the ripples of these actions. Just like the baby who discards a new gift, we quickly tire of our new toys and anticipate owning 'version III' - we're easily bored. In our hearts we know these things are transient; they're merely a 'consolation prize' for something else - something that eludes us until we 'have the time' to start looking for it. Until then, we wipe out any notions about the 'truth' of our existence because we can't access it right 'now' - it's too concealed and been corrupted. Being 'too busy' is a way of distracting ourselves or allowing ourselves to be distracted by others - we fill the 'black hole' with possessions and empty pursuits. We look for contentment without even thinking about what it means to be content - it always means gratification of desire in our society. A piece of chocolate cake lasts for minutes, an ancient monument perhaps for thousands of years, but neither can ever be permanent.

There are different types of desire - physical and non-physical (spiritual, metaphysical or abstract - whichever term you prefer). The pleasure we receive from fulfilling our desires is temporary; it's like trying to repair holes in the road with ice - it soon melts revealing the hole again. The succession of unsuccessful repairs to the road surface leaves us feeling frustrated and inadequate - so it is with any gratification of desire. Until we realise this, it's impossible to live in harmony with ourselves and by extension, with each other. We look for completeness without knowing what it means - looking for it in relationships (with an individual or within a group) or on the stacked shelves of commercialism. Both of these are closely connected to the security we wish to find, but neither can handle the task. There's absolutely nothing anyone can obtain outside of themselves that will cause them to feel happy or complete for the rest of their lives - nothing that will fill the void. We can only find this completeness by a process of negation; a process that first finds out why we 'desire' so much and why, beneath the skin of our physical existence, we feel so empty.

Am I Good Enough?

*Find out why you feel the way you feel -
about yourself.*

The answer to the question 'Am I good enough?' depends on who we ask. If we ask ourselves, then generally the answer is 'No'. If we ask someone else and they say 'Yes', we tend not to believe them. Am I good enough? Yes! Absolutely! We're all good enough. Then why don't we feel it? Because of continual encouragement and manipulation to believe otherwise. I could end this chapter here, but I want to write further on the topic, as it's a particularly difficult problem to overcome, and I'm still working on it. It's not enough to be told 'Yes! Absolutely! We're all good enough' - words are a thin blanket against the cold. When society repeatedly hammers in 'not good enough' messages, like splinters, they have to be removed before they do more damage; however, we can't look to our 'tormenter' for assistance - we must remove them ourselves. To put this another way - because I want to stress the point - the path we trod to feeling not good enough was a tough one, and it's just as difficult to come off it. Splinters hurt like hell when we try to remove them, particularly when we have to dig deep to get them out.

Every time we look into the mirror we answer 'No' to the question 'Am I good enough?', even though we spend hours putting on makeup and our hard-earned pennies on a new outfit or hairdo. We invest in looking good on the outside but rather sadly, also in feeling bad. We go to great pains to make ourselves attractive and acceptable, not just for the sake of others, but to make ourselves feel better. This effort gets us through the day/evening but, in the morning - the beast is back - our hair is a frightful mess and we're our-awful-selves again - our faithful mirror confirms this. I know there are those of us who 'throw' our clothes on and don't bother with the rituals, but most do; either way, most of us would like to 'tweak' what we see, whether it's to lose or gain a few pounds, have curly hair instead of straight, be a little taller, shorter, have slimmer waists or thinner thighs. Some of us aren't averse to having major surgery performed or even a 'total body transplant' (our own mind in the body of one of the icons we idolise). Several people have told me that they're perfectly happy with themselves and even that they love their reflection in the mirror, but they take the trouble to be stylish and wear makeup. 'Makeup' implies making up for a lack of some kind; it's a decoration that covers up what's beautiful and natural about us. No matter how well we dress up or how many layers of makeup we put on, we don't feel any different on the inside. We return home after our excursions to face the same walls and ornaments - nothing changes behind the security of our barriers. Physically, we've become more comfortable behind screens and masks than we are in our 'natural' state. We feel increasingly safe behind our various electronic screens and don't need to get dressed to enter into our virtual world - safe in the knowledge that the images on our profile - out-of-date or otherwise - will adequately 'clothe' us.

However, on another level, we're at our most comfortable at home alone when we take off our disguises. We're much happier lounging around barefoot in joggers without the need to keep up appearances or conform to the expectations of society by wearing a suit - or other uniform - to work for example - not to do so is unacceptable in many workplaces. We pretend to be happy with our lives and in some minor ways we are; however, nagging in the back of our minds - like a dripping tap - are doubts and questions about why we agree to behave in these ways. We spend our lives supporting beliefs that we're not good enough, and tend to surround ourselves 'subconsciously' with people who confirm it. One reason for this is that we love to fall into the fantasy of the different characters we're capable of becoming; we're brilliant at it, but need a supporting cast or audience in order to keep it up. As new fashions are offered up to us, so are the complimentary labels that go with them; such as, hell's angels, punks, goths or whatever the latest genre is. Unfortunately, our cultures encourage us to veer more in the direction of trendy and need. The personalities that 'go with' new fashions - to those who don't follow them - are rarely 'angelic' and usually to be feared when they're in groups; these groups cause further division in society. The costumes, traits and fears were created by someone else and therefore, can't be natural to us. I added 'need' to the above statement, because we all need to find out who we are; we seek a true identity and the commercials play on this. I'd suggest that any character is a limited creation, because we zoom into particular personality traits that become who we think we are; for example:

- Free-spirited
- Workaholic
- Sociable
- Daredevil
- Law-abiding
- Criminal
- Sporty
- Tough
- Religious
- Adventurous
- Sophisticated (please research this word - it means impure/un-natural)

These are creations of the Mind and from them we've created our society. Besides choosing which outfit to wear each day (and how) they're not new and not our own creations but merely a 'mix and match' of what we already have. We can change a colour, add studs or cut slits in the knees of our jeans, but none of it is new; in Tudor times, for example, 'slashed' clothing was fashionable, revealing what was being worn beneath a particular layer. Once we attach ourselves to these personality labels they stick and become what other people expect us to be and subconsciously, who we think we are until, if ever, we decide to change our costumes. To put this another way, we're walking along the catwalk modelling clothes and images that someone else has designed for us. It's rare that apart from very close friends we'd allow anyone to see us without our makeup or 'slumming it' at home. We keep up the façade but our true nature is divine - wide-angled and limitless - if it wasn't we wouldn't be able to act out these parts. For example, no-one is born a goth or punk; we learn how to play these roles and love doing it. We're capable of playing all parts and we do; however, these roles are being cast for us - we're being 'directed'. To sum up this point, we have an innate need to have the question 'Who am I?' answered and when society tells us, you're a 'goth', 'rocker', 'bookworm', 'sex-bomb', 'nerd', 'genius', whatever - we go along with it. In truth, we fall into 'not good enough' mode when we stitch ourselves to one label and that label becomes the limit of our comfort zones - those limits become our prisons. It's more worthwhile to find out who we're not than it is to believe any label - negation is highly productive; for example, 'what' or 'who' are these labels attached to is worth pondering.

I've written much about topics that we don't particularly want to examine; they're not pleasing to our ears, because they make us feel that we 'ought' to make changes in our lives and we don't want the disruption. However, we can't find truth unless we're prepared to question our reality and in questioning reality it's important not to answer those questions. The reason for this is that we can only answer them from the same conditioning that gave us answers up to now; in other words, from the unhealthy Mind that is the river we all live in. Our education was never about who we are and it never encouraged us to find out either; it filled our heads with an abundance of information that was about everything but us, and what would be expected from us in the future. As a result we're unable to find out who we are from our 'knowledge base'. It's no wonder that humanity is puzzled about its origin and purpose; we don't have a clue who we are, or how we got ourselves into this mess. As long as we defend a society that in our hearts we know is sick, we won't be able to see the possibilities that lie beyond it.

As I've said before, we try to answer the question 'Who am I?' by looking outside of ourselves instead of in - it's a spiritual question. When we reply to the question physically we can never get the right answer and there are two ways in which we try to do this. Firstly, by altering our physical structure through leisure activities such as sports - particularly those that build muscles to a point where we become unrecognisable to ourselves or others; we also do this through surgery, and at the minor end of the scale by changing the way we dress, having a 'makeover' or taking on some other persona. Regardless of the methods we use to disguise ourselves, inside we haven't changed at all - it's entirely superficial. Secondly, we attempt to succeed by climbing a 'ladder'. Who are the 'chairman', 'president', gold medallist or a 'scientist' without their labels, and what is left for them to 'achieve' when they wear them? The trouble with the top of a ladder is that it comes to an end, abruptly. There are only three things we can do from the top of a ladder; stay there, climb down or fall off it - the ladder of society is a dead end. Okay, some may argue that you can jump off (or be pushed), but these actions lead to the same unhappy ending - an eventual fall from a powerful yet fragile illusion that our egos don't want to let go of. I'd suggest, we can never become anything other than who we really are (as opposed to who we think we are), and that we dabble with life by trying on different masks and living in ways that keep up and reinforce the pretence.

I had a friend who took these masks to extremes and her personality and accent changed regularly, even with me. We were reasonably well-spoken when we were children (I don't like these scales, but this was our conditioning). I can still remember the time I heard her speak, using profanities, in another accent altogether; she wanted to fit in with the friend she was with at the time and I was expected to go along with it, which I didn't. She perfected her styles to fit into any social environment she found herself in and, as is inevitable when we experiment to this extreme, became increasingly confused about her own identity to the point where, under some circumstances, even I didn't recognise her. For the record, I've no problem with anyone speaking in any accent or any way they want to, but when these get mixed together - as with my friend - it becomes difficult, if not impossible, to relate to them. Surely our relationships with each other are confusing enough without increasing the confusion of the relationship we learn to have with ourselves. If you'd been born in England you'd think of yourself as English, but if the same 'you' had been born in Russia instead, you would have become an entirely different person, with a different set of cultural beliefs and expectations - the root is the same, but the branches are different.

~~~

There's something nebulous about answering the question 'Am I good enough?' - it has a vagueness we can't quite put our finger on. Missing from the question is what or who we ought to be good enough for. Interestingly, more often than not we tell ourselves 'I'm not good enough' and that, let's face it, slams our don't go there door in our own face - eliminating the question altogether. Being 'not good enough' was the root of what prevented me from writing for so many years; however, putting my mind to doing what I love became a cure for that. I'm good enough to do many more things too, but they'd be half-hearted distractions that would prevent me from following what I now accept as being my 'path'. A big obstacle to overcome is the belief that we can't earn a living from doing what we want to do but it can be overcome - only fear constructs the boundaries that enclose us. We can never know what'll happen if we decide to follow our dreams until we take action, but we live in fear of the unborn and conditioned consequences nevertheless. This is like standing by a door and being afraid to open it, just in case there's something nasty on the other side waiting to pounce.

Who is the tormentor I mentioned earlier in this chapter and why would they want to hammer us with 'not good enough' messages - so much so, that we feel terrible about ourselves and have to hide behind a cast of characters in a play that quite clearly we can't see we're not the directors of? That sounds like a loaded question - and it is - but please don't try to answer without thinking about it. There are many levels to this question, but as always I only look at what I can see clearly and have meditated on myself. When we turn our attention inwards and cease to look outside for answers then the identity of our tormentor becomes obvious - it's ourselves. We torment ourselves day and night - so much so that we have to keep busy in order to get away from the 'noise'; however, it's still going on subconsciously. I won't even try to answer the 'why' part of the question because we can't know the answer to it; nevertheless, it's a question we ask.

We need only observe our mind to see how negative and antagonistic it is, and how it leads us into states of mind that aren't good for us such as arguments, anger, aggression, low self-esteem, fear, shyness and addiction. I'd suggest that to some extent at least, our characters are inborn and further develop as we grow, according to the environment we grow up in; in my case this was an orphanage, and not at all pleasant. When they stopped punishing me for my existence I took over, because I didn't know anything else; I wasn't conscious of this phenomenon at the time. We tend to take over the roles of our past tormentors, or go on to torment others - either way is self-destructive and passes these habits onto future generations. We torment ourselves, far more than anyone else ever did; we're self-punishing and our own harshest critics. All our pain comes from stored memories and when we observe this fact closely it becomes clearer and clearer. We can't erase the memories, but we can put them into context and see them for what they really are - the past, which no longer exists (personally, I question whether it ever did). When we try to 'locate' our painful memories, we can't - it's like trying to locate a dream. What we learn from these past experiences, and what we're prepared to tackle or change, is entirely up to us.

If we want to change we can. The road is difficult because the Mind resists at every twist and turn; it likes to keep us on our familiar track of self-destruction. With honest reflection and close examination of ourselves this can be overcome; we need an unshakable 'will' never to give up. How many of us have bought self-help books in the past and felt on a 'high' after reading them? The 'hit' from these books can be temporary because:

- They tend not to go deeply enough into what's happening inside our heads/minds.
- We don't realise that we have to do more than just 'read the book' and then shelve it.
- We tend to use the information to advise others rather than apply it to ourselves; we're very good at this.
- There's no quick fix and this can be discouraging - like a diet we give up on.
- A 'hit' is just that; like when a ball hits a wall it bounces off again, and we're not prepared for this.

We buy these books because deep inside of each of us is a need to find out who we are, and in self-help books we share the experiences of others, in the hope that we'll find our way out of the despair and confusion our world is full of. No matter how good a self-help book is or how full our bookshelves are, if we're not ready to change, it's not going to happen. Generally, all we find is more confusion as self-help has become an 'industry'; we try to get to grips with the thousands of - mostly recycled - 'infallible' systems for 'healing' ourselves. The 'determination' and 'will' not to give up come on their own, once we see that the path we're currently walking on leads nowhere. When we see this, changing paths becomes not only worthwhile, but essential and with this comes our passion to keep 'walking' - giving up, is no longer an option.

~~~

When we try to reach unattainable goals they leave us feeling 'not good enough'. For example, we may visit our hairdresser and choose a hairstyle from one of their magazines; despite being advised that it won't suit us, we go ahead. Once created, it feels like a knock-back - we still don't look like the model, because we don't have the same face or colouring. I remember when I was around fifteen and feeling particularly inadequate. I bought a blonde hair dye kit and - without reflection - used it; my hair turned orange (I really mean orange). My head looked like the top of a Belisha beacon when I'd finished. I looked such a fright that I had to return immediately to the chemist (headscarf on) to buy a bottle of black hair dye in an attempt to get back to my own colour. It's ridiculous to try to become somebody else based on an image we've seen. Another example of how we do this is to buy the clothes a model looks great in and then hit ourselves hard when we don't look as 'good' in the same outfit. We bring up our children to follow 'heroes' and 'success' images, which is how they become as confused and insecure as we are. We can't walk in the footsteps of another person, nor along their path; we must each find our own way, but as long as we live our lives like obedient copycats or lookalikes we can't realistically expect to find out who we are, or what we'd be capable of if we were in control. At this point, I find myself wondering just how many Michael Jackson or Elvis impersonators there are in the world. To walk along someone else's path, is to completely disregard our own existence or purpose.

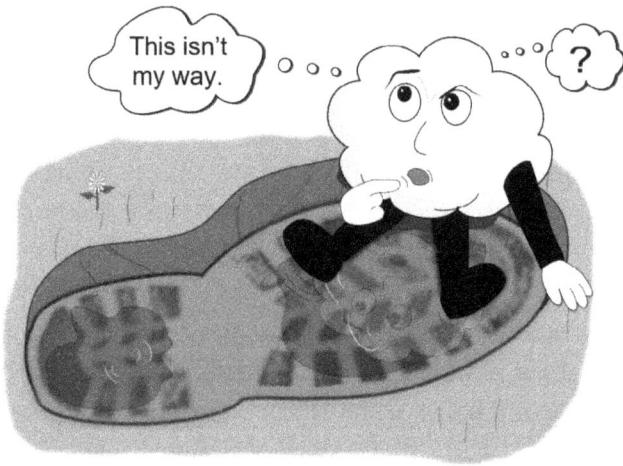

If we stop believing there's something greater than ourselves, that led us to where we are now, what've we got left? We're tiny in the universe, but have been given a great deal of responsibility in it - at least on this 'earth'. We're so busy wallowing in feeling bad about ourselves and re-living our pasts that we can't see the wonder of our existence - a physical manifestation of something metaphysical - more marvellous than we're capable of imagining. The world suffers with low self-esteem, because it insists on repeating - and ignoring the ramifications of - its past mistakes. We live in fear of change - thereby resisting it - and at the same time, we long for it. An argument or conflict only come into being when we have opposing agendas with ourselves or others. Two of these common arguments are 'I'm not good enough' or 'someone else isn't good enough'. We sabotage our happiness and peace because we don't believe we deserve it; we live on the edge playing in our 'one-man-band' with full knowledge that it's being orchestrated from the outside. We effectively destroy the opportunity to find a better life for ourselves when we insist on remaining in 'not good enough' mode, which is only a perversion of who we truly are. It's tough - very tough, but if we see that the burden is spread over the whole of humanity, it lightens our load. When we see this clearly then we feel the pains of others before feeling our own; in other words, we no longer see the world subjectively but realise that we are the world, and everything we think and do is reflected in it. The only thing we believe we're not good enough for is ourselves and one reason for this is that we're not ready to take responsibility for our freedom. The path is long, dark and tough, but it is there and there is 'light' at the end of it; beyond that light, who can really know what we'll find. We overcome all hurdles when we no longer get distracted or deterred by society. When we become the act instead of the audience many doors open, but we have to make the first move and be serious about our quest, which at first, can appear to be a hopeless task; however, if we continue on it, it becomes clear that it isn't.

Responsibility

Everything is as it should be, but not as it could be.

Responsibility, as we tend to understand it, means being answerable for the actions or inactions of ourselves or others, such as our children, employees or neighbours; however, in reality, responsibility has come to be understood as an ability to manage 'obligations' that society has put upon us. Responsibility is a mantle we grow into when we're 'old enough' - old enough to look after a younger sibling, to earn a living, drive a car, buy a home, get married or start a family. Sometimes we're forced to assume the role of a mantle earlier than expected - perhaps due to the death of a parent. We become responsible for getting to work on time, driving safely and teaching our children to be 'well-behaved' so they fit in with society - keeping those cogs turning; the process is mechanical. In theory, this leads to a happy and rewarding life, but in practise our dreams lie unfulfilled, financial commitments increase, wages don't keep pace and our children's interests lie outside the family home (either physically or online), leaving us somewhat obsolete in their eyes, as they live in a world that we 'apparently' know nothing about. Our societal responsibilities have become a heavy burden, and once they're 'fulfilled' we tend to feel prematurely retired and rather at a loss for what to do with ourselves. While carrying out our 'responsibilities' life whizzed by, and we strayed far from the true meaning of responsibility - the ability to respond, as opposed to pre-conditioned responses that rely on thought and therefore, memory.

Though we complain about monotony and the problems in our world, we tend to accept it all as an inevitable 'way of life'. Society expects nothing less and we accept the 'contingency plans' it puts forward for us; for example, retirement homes, pensions and bus passes. However, history teaches us that we are and always have been stagnant - psychologically - and despite the horrors that have resulted, we refuse to change our ways regardless of the cost of this apathy; the cost is to accept the authority of others, which we willingly do, no matter how they use or misuse it. We've place a huge burden on the back of a donkey and expect that donkey to carry our load, but it never makes our load lighter - it increases the weight and leaves us feeling powerless, because under these circumstances we are powerless. By accepting the authority (guidance) of another, by definition, we make them our 'Master' and relinquish our right to think for ourselves - we lose the ability to reason and to know that there are other choices. We leave our burden on the back of the donkey who is quite willing to carry it - for a price.

Throughout taught history, humanity has been violent and willing to fight in immoral wars that leave a trail of devastation; we learn nothing from them and have no idea what we're really fighting for anyway. The order is 'shoot' and we obey - this is madness. We're far removed from taking responsibility for the carnage and destruction this fragmentation of humanity causes; in a twist, we shed responsibility while claiming to act in its cause; however, the action we take is superficial, in a way that society has made 'correct'. Mostly, this 'correct' way is to take no action and leave everything to our elected 'authorities', but also to apply dressings to the wounds of our victims and environment, whilst crying over them - our tears falling into collection boxes of one sort or another. How much easier it is to cry about something we can do nothing about, than something we can. We look to society - which created our problems - to solve them, because we don't want to take on that responsibility ourselves for more than say, picking up litter or recycling our waste; we're far too busy being 'busy'. However, we are that society. In the above two examples, it makes more sense to put our litter straight into bins and more importantly, not to create so much waste in the first place - the solutions are always easy if we take responsibility, and we can do this under our own authority - it's empowering. We can get so cross with the dustmen when they go on strike and don't pick up our rubbish - it's worth thinking about this. We produce far more waste than the authorities can cope with or will take away, yet still we demand increasingly efficient services for our increasing volume of landfill material. Our responsibilities surely must go further than this - to at least think about what happens to this rubbish after it's out of our sight. Just because we can no longer see it, doesn't mean that it's no longer there.

It's absurd to think that we're powerless to create a better world, in which the whole of humanity has enough food and is happy; we don't even have to create it, as there's already enough for every one of us. To believe that suffering is inevitable is a limit put forward by the voice of our egos, not the voice of rational or compassionate thought. Even more absurd is that we agree to live in a world filled with violence, greed and apathy - dumping responsibility for it onto elected governments that we hope will change things for us. We can't hope to become responsible whilst placing responsibility in the hands of other people who are also irresponsible. Governments are a part of our unhealthy society and made up of human beings just like us - they don't know any more about the nature of the world we live in than we do, and they're certainly no wiser. We've been diverted from our beautiful world and lured into the worlds of others - worlds that are highly immoral and far from benevolent. It's humanity who complies with this diversion and sits quietly watching and crying about the destruction seen either on news broadcasts, or as an eye-witness in so-called third-world countries - then we move in and clean up the mess. However, we only create more mess, hatred, bitterness and division in this process. Imagine an enclosed room in which we dust and sweep the floors; all we really do is move the dirt from one place to another; the room can never be cleaned, until someone opens a window and allows in light and fresh air. We've lost our ability to reason and are living in a world of common nonsense, rather than common sense.

~~~

The intention of this chapter is not to 'tell off' humanity - there would be no point in that. I too am part of that society and see clearly that for the most part of my life I did nothing to change it - nothing to change 'me'. However, now that I see this I can't sit by and do nothing; more importantly, I know I can't rely on others to change anything for me. We were born into this mess, and therefore it's hard to see how we can get out of it - it's also difficult to see how we got into it. This chapter is a plea to humanity to - at least - begin to see the folly of our ways, how we've inherited this mindset and how we're leaving it as a legacy to our children. One tiny footstep towards understanding the mindset of humanity, is a huge step in the right direction. We can't make plans to live in better ways because they won't work; the plans would be made by the society that created the problems, and we know that when society makes plans things get more complicated, rather than simpler. We're re-formatting old information to try to find something new; all we're going to find inside a haystack, is hay. We only need to recognise what's going on - in good conscience - and the rest takes care of itself. If we take those 'Huh!' and 'What the heck!' moments one step further when something seems to be odd or ridiculous, rather than brushing them aside, we start a process that picks up its own momentum; it is, however, up to us to keep that momentum going, or let it grind to a halt. We need to recognise and consider why our world is being abused, before casting aspersions about who's responsible for it.

We live in a world where good news is not welcome, where those who spread love and morality are ostracised; it's a world where everything is up-side-down and impossible to comprehend or get to the bottom of, and a world where the bottom of the ladder (immorality and corruption) is considered to be the top. This situation is not 'new' - it's been spoken about for millennia and still we aren't listening. We feel helpless, unworthy and are in pain to the point of despair; only fear keeps us rooted to the spot - fear of the things we believe we can't change, and the things we can. In other words, we fear 'change' itself - we don't want to upset the apple cart. There's little for us to do for our 'entertainment' and 'amusement' other than to watch programs (social media too) that mock others, offer prizes, bring bad news, promote violence, immorality, ignorance and stupidity - dumbing down a willing and obeisant society. Alternatively, we can drink or drug ourselves into oblivion, act outrageously, become obsessed with our bodies, shop ourselves silly or compete with each other. The greatest entertainment of all comes from our own mind - our true elected authority. We can protest about what's going on, but a protest is only a request for somebody else to change something. It's no wonder that 'hope' holds no power over us, let alone faith - it's not a good position to be in. We tend to work in directions that increase our salaries - if we have a job at all - in order to pay our increasing bills; this is a material world. We work in pointless jobs that serve the system we complain about - and rely on - because we can't see the way out of all the confusion and kerfuffle that get in the way. In this world, we're for or against the system, but whatever our preference we tend to believe ourselves powerless to change it. We're not powerless at all - it just feels that way when we look at it from a subjective and 'locked-in' point of view - when we don't want, or know how, to take responsibility for our own lives.

~~~

The first step to becoming responsible is to realise how much responsibility we've put onto others; such as, governments for bringing peace to the world, teachers for the education of our children, religions for 'guidance', science for 'solutions' and a 'justice' system to keep law and order. None of these would be necessary or even exist but for the fragmentation of our world; the cause creates the effect, but the effect doesn't bring an end to the cause - it generates more of it. We don't have to look far to see that there's no peace, that society is largely being dumbed down and that we live without 'guidance' or justice - none of these are heading in a positive direction. None of the above authorities are healthy themselves so we can't reasonably expect them to solve the problems of humanity; they are humanity. The world is different when we look at these scenarios from a distance. Becoming responsible is a process - a process of self-observation and examination that leads to a better understanding of ourselves and therefore, what it means to be responsible - it's also realising how irresponsible we actually are.

The biggest argument against becoming responsible is that we believe if one person changes, they can't change the whole - an 'everybody's doing it' excuse - so we drop out of responsibility and join the masses; I had big issues with this one. The problem needs to be faced before we can see the bigger picture and before we realise what a huge difference a change of perspective can make. Too often we want to know results before we even look at problems and this is the result of learning by rote; when we learn by rote we don't learn at all - we memorise. I can't tell you how it feels to reach the age of fifty, because you wouldn't be able to relate to my experiences; we have to wait for our own birthday. In so many ways, reaching the age of fifty changes our lives - mostly because of conditioning - regardless of what the rest of the world is up to. Humanity is arrogant to think that it already understands, knows and believes itself to be in control of the universe it lives in. One person changing the 'whole' only seems to be impossible, until we make more than a passing effort to try it.

~~~

I infrequently refer to, but never discuss religion or politics in my books as these subjects are responsible for so much of humanity's pain and confusion. Instead, I prefer to erase all conditioning - by seeing it for what it is and looking at the world through unveiled eyes. I received several responses to my 'Thank You' page in a previous book, regarding my thank you to 'God' and it has caused some people to say 'She's God Squad'; how closed-minded we can be when we accept the conditioning of society, and judge others inflexibly, without seeing the whole picture. This is a trained mechanical reaction - it lacks independent and rational thought. These rejections are our resistance to letting go of our problems; we tend to refuse to hear or see anything that might help us. This may be because we've been let down by society before and even though our reaction isn't good for us, it's all we have for security; we know - only from our own perspective - where we stand with it. Look closely at this and it's easy to see that 'God Squad' is nothing but a well-worn cliché and that these three letters (God) are enough to break up friendships, start wars and drag us into the realms of so-called 'darkness', where we can live safely in fear; just three letters can do all that and more. Another friend of mine associated the word God with 'organised religion'. God, on my 'thank you' page is short for Godfrey - a friend that gave me so much encouragement to finish my books. I've now changed 'God' to 'Godfrey'; I changed it because I want to reach as many people as possible and if they close the book without getting past the front matter, then I'll change that front matter -

this is my responsibility and obligation, but only if the hurdle agrees with my reason. I don't feel responsible for other people's problems or for picking up the pieces of their lives, but I do feel responsible for doing what I can through my books - it's my world after all. The alternative was to dig in my heels and allow myself to be controlled by my ego and pride which is always counter-productive. Many years ago I would've done just that, as then I felt responsible only for sustaining the tightly enclosing illusions that defined who I believed myself to be; these are the 'notes' we pin on the walls of our minds and refuse to remove. Does God exist? This is a question worth pondering, but only if we get rid of every thought and belief about it currently entrenched on our minds; we can never find truth in subjects that have been influenced by others and consequently, labelled 'taboo'. We're far more powerful than we dare to believe. No matter how rich or poor, how educated or how many books we've read, we can know all we'll ever need to know, only by searching inside ourselves.

~~~

If we're old enough to say 'Yes' to something, then surely we're old enough to say 'No' as well; however, we tend to make these decisions based on conditioning rather than wisdom, which is why we make so many 'mistakes' in our lives. When I was seventeen I married for the first time; the decision was made based on fairytale happy endings, parental/societal consent and a need to leave my family home; no wisdom, responsibility or reason came into my decision - I most certainly wasn't ready for such a commitment or subsequent ones many years later.

I was playing life 'by the rules'. We tend to take our first 'drink' when we 'come of age' - sometimes pretending we've reached it earlier - and it can't be denied that this and other minimum age limits are entirely conditioned. We're told when we've reached 'grown up' status and are generally far from responsible once we reach this milestone. I'd suggest grown up status isn't grown up at all, if by 'grown up' we mean 'coming 'of age' - coming of age is not an indicator of psychological maturity, and in no way implies being responsible.

Becoming responsible begins with an honest 'change of mind' - our mind. When this happens, it's amazing to watch it in 'action' and catch ourselves out when we're up to mischief; when we look at and judge another person, when we're about to tell a lie to ourselves - or to someone else - or when we get a glimpse of our reflection in the mirror and recognise a familiar moment of vanity. We become aware of our contradictory and irrational behaviour; we know when to say 'yes' when our mind says 'no', and 'no' when it says 'yes'. When we become responsible for ourselves, we become deeply aware of our surroundings, the movement of our thoughts, and of the same true nature of every human being, without any division or judgement. Everything falls into place in its own time, but only if we want it to. If we remain self-observant and self-critical, riding the inevitable ups and downs of these activities, we allow in that welcome 'light' and 'fresh air', and invite grace, humility and wisdom to guide us.

Consolidation

*Before becoming One with humanity
we have to become One with ourselves.*

The title for this chapter came to me in the middle of the night. I woke up remembering a time, when I had so many different email addresses and messenger nicknames, that I had to be careful about who I was speaking to and how; it was rather confusing when multi-tasking, or talking to more than one person at a time. I'd frequently send messages, in error, to the wrong person; I think we've all done this at some point in our lives, and these momentary lapses of concentration can be awkward, if not embarrassing. They occurred in the days when instant messaging was relatively new, and we were encouraged - more so now - to be fearful of the people we'd encounter online; we could only message from desktop computers at that time. I had to keep notes of my nicknames and passwords because there were too many to remember by heart. I could 'hide' from some people while showing online to others and have to admit, it was rather fun and empowering; I had some bad experiences, true, but also met some lovely people with whom I'm still in contact. Not much has changed, except that we can now do all these things on different devices and websites - the charade is more wide-angled. Naïvely, many still believe that if they keep things 'private' online, no-one will know who or where they are. We may think we're invisible, but are easily 'seen' - by those who want to see us - as long as we remain permanently logged in to, and communicating through our various devices.

The illusion of anonymity is rapidly disappearing as social media websites tend to encourage us to use the better_known@email_addresses.whatever to any that may be more personal such as those connected to our own domains. As we 'log in', our personal details and contacts are ripped out of our - what we thought to be private - contact list and added to the new site; the larger websites are becoming more and more closely connected to each other, resulting in us logging into multiple sites with just one click; convenient, 'Yes!'; in our best interest, 'No!'. Whether we like it or not, the cloud is expanding and enveloping us, by our acceptance of its invitation. We're not always explicitly asked if it's okay for the people who run these websites to copy our contacts, but it's often in those brilliant long-winded 'terms and conditions' that we click 'agree' on; who has the time or inclination to read them? To add to the intrusion, these websites then make suggestions for further contacts we might like to add based on the contacts of the contacts they copied; what other information have they gathered? It's all part of a long-term process of 'consolidation' (control) on the internet and off.

However, this type of consolidation is not what interests me and it's not really what this chapter is about. I mention it because it's a good model for the kind of consolidation that does interest me; the journey that each and every one of us will one day make - becoming One with ourselves; it's a process that begins by accepting the things we have no power to change, and expending our energy on that which we can do something about - ourselves. Becoming One with myself and humanity interests me, but becoming One with the insane and immoral society we've created, doesn't. In both cases we don't know who is in control, but in one case we can find out. When we realise this, we have a choice - remain in ignorance, or change.

~~~

Some of the things I was told as a child left me puzzled, like 'Snap out of it', 'Get a grip of yourself', 'Pull your socks up' or 'Pull yourself together'. The latter in particular left me somewhat bewildered as it seemed to me that I wasn't in pieces. Looking back, it now makes sense; more so, I would imagine, than it meant to the people who used to say it - the ones who delighted in taking me apart at such a tender age. As a child, teenager and young adult - way into my thirties - I played many roles for different audiences. We all do it (some more than others) as it's in our nature - our conditioned nature. There was the 'me' that spoke to family, to friends, another to work colleagues, another 'me' to my doctor, father, self in the mirror, people I didn't like and a 'me' reserved for the complaints departments in shops - I took pride in each one. There were also the 'me's' that developed the characters for my online aliases, but in those cases I gave them monikers too. All these 'me's' were like the branches of a tree - reaching out in different directions from one trunk. I wasn't aware of any of this at the time, but now realise I was 'divided', confused, incoherent and had no idea who 'me' was.

We put on different characters, for different people, but we don't do it for fun; in most cases we do it subconsciously, and automatically, as we're so used to it. We hide parts of who we think we are, and develop the parts of who we wish to be or whatever fits any given situation the best - from the various role models we encounter in one way or another. For example, I was good at complaining in shops and getting refunds for goods I was returning, but knowing what I know now, my immaturity was obvious and I probably got the refunds just so they could get rid of me - I was rather aggressive. In order to do this successfully I must have watched others doing it and tried to assert myself in the same way. My characters concealed a far deeper insecurity that was afraid of the world (my world) and I hid behind them, pretending that the insecurity didn't exist - giving the illusion of me standing up for my 'rights' - 'the mouse that roared'. It seems strange that I could act the part out, but not make it a part of my 'private' self; however, it works because when we act out these parts we reinforce the walls we don't wish others to see through; we don't like the traits we hide about ourselves, and so we cover them up with layers that please us more. I don't believe we do this to deceive, but rather to survive and also because deep down we've come to love playing 'let's pretend' - literally losing ourselves in the new characters we create or rather, assemble. I created what I believed I lacked and at the same time, protected myself in case it went wrong; I kept what I believed to be my true self 'Private and Confidential' - well hidden.

Gradually, new personas are created from our assembled traits, including our body language, speech and temperament. We spend many years tweaking these until who we really are becomes so deeply buried under personas, conditioning, wishes, hopes, pains, fears and frustrations that we don't know who we are anymore - if we ever did. If you give this some thought for a while, with an open mind, it becomes apparent that our multi-faceted characters have been entirely created and are being maintained, by us, or rather by our minds and egos. Behind all the layers of 'pretence' lies something else. For this reason 'Who am I?' is the most important question we can ponder and generally, it can only be approached by being prepared to remove all our artificial coverings and stripping ourselves back to bare plaster, as it were.

Like layers of old wallpaper, these layers of conditioning aren't easily stripped off. One reason for this is that there's no reward for doing so; 'What's in it for me?' is a non-starter and nothing can replace the layers or prevent our inevitable resulting vulnerability. This might feel like a waste of time but I can assure you it isn't. It's these layers that hold us in our 'prisons' and therefore, when we remove them we remove fears, pains and frustrations - it sets us free. For those of you who have long hair you know how difficult it can be to remove the tangles. You can't begin from the top of your head because the lower tangles get worse and the whole process becomes painful. We have to begin from the ends and gradually work our way up - it's much easier in the long run and when we do this regularly our hair shines and is in much better condition. There are times however, when we reach particularly stubborn tangles or awkward pieces of wallpaper and it's easy to become disheartened. It's the same process for removing our layers - gradually our pains and frustrations peel away with them; it's these layers that have caused all our confusion. I say gradually, but in reality, we sometimes let go of a lot all at once. It takes concerted effort and determination to 'come clean' with ourselves, and at times this can be hilarious and humbling. For example, if I have a disagreement with a friend and our 'layers' reveal their ugly heads again, we now tend to burst out laughing in recognition of what's happening and let it all pass over. It's much more fun than being two angry bulls head-to-head in the middle of a no-win argument, which only serves to create more layers of grudges, anger, hatred or whatever you will.

Untangling hair and removing layers of wallpaper are useful metaphors to help explain what's involved in the process of consolidation, but on a practical level they leave us somewhat baffled; they are 'outside' physical actions that we need to apply to a spiritual concept. The difficulty comes in trying to translate these metaphors into a metaphysical 'action' for a mind that has never given it any serious thought and in my case at least, it took many years to see. The concept is alien to us - we haven't been conditioned this way; on the contrary, we've been taught that outside action brings results. We've been taught that the world is physical and our spiritual nature has been ignored; we're not encouraged to think about what life is about, what we're doing here or why we're always at war - nothing changes.

~~~

I mentioned in an earlier chapter, 'Our Cluttered Mind', a friend who cleared out his attic - letting go of some old memories at the same time. Now, perhaps this is going to sound insane to you, but there's nothing we need to physically do; observation and recognition of how we constructed ourselves and society are what's needed to start the process. Society is a reflection of our layers and what we've buried beneath them; our world is a reflection of the mind of that society. The insane mind created our insane society and society, the insane world; surely it's time to put this vehicle into reverse by 'unlearning'. Once we see through the illusion it falls away by itself. However, it's generally difficult for us to see how to make changes to anything without physical action. For example:

- Our house will remain dirty unless we clean it.
- We can't get anywhere without moving our feet or on some other mode of transport.
- We can't get a worthwhile job unless we pass our exams.
- We can't buy anything without handing over money.
- We can't have full stomachs unless we eat.

We're in the habit of having to do something in the physical world in order to see 'results'. Our characters hang on our branches which hang on a tree trunk and our lives are dependent on a social conditioning system that's controlled by our apathy; we blame this control on so-called 'fat cats', but they only get fat on what we feed them. Our desires feed our society and we'll sacrifice much in order to satisfy them; for example, our spiritual journey or a debt-free life, in order to buy something like a house, a car or the latest mobile phone. The physical is a projection of what's going on in our minds; we're separated, in pain, sorrowful, confused, proud and angry. These feelings lead to wars of all types in our world, but these wars will never end, because we're fighting each other, rather than thinking about why we won't stop doing it. The first war that needs to be brought to an end is the one going on inside our head.

Our conditioning makes metaphysical exploration difficult; we can't conceive of anything outside of the physical other than what we've been taught, shown in films or read in books. There's so much (physical) that we refuse to let go of because of fear that - for example, we might need it one day. All this has to be put out of our minds if we're to see a bigger picture. We don't have to leave our homes or give up our jobs; we only have to begin to look at things in a different way and become aware of the conditioning that influences our thoughts and actions. If our lives are meant to change in the process, then they will without any help from us; the universe works in strange ways that we don't yet understand and maybe never will. Though we don't need to take physical action there are ways in which it helps. We can take a look around our homes and see how much we've accumulated over the years; this can be shocking when we realise that the inside of our homes - to a large extent if not entirely - represents the inside of our mind. All our memories and sentiments surround us and we're reluctant to let go of them - so it is with conditioning. We mirror our minds in our homes and now also on the internet, and the contents of these mirror the baggage we're not prepared to let go of. We're reluctant to let go because our conditioning, homes and belongings represent who we think we are; they serve to define us and therefore are the boundary between the physical and the metaphysical, or if you will, our spiritual nature. There's nothing wrong with having things - it's when those things have us that our problems begin.

The strength and fight we put up to keep these things secured in our homes, and memories is formidable - sentimentality and fear are powerful forces, but they can be overcome by first recognising our 'state', and then having the will to act on that knowledge. It's this act of recognition that releases us from our beliefs that they're a part of who we are. The layers, previously mentioned, won't peel away easily but they can be removed if we're sincere in our intentions. For example, bringing a multitude of media pages together as one; this process begins to set us free from our multi-faceted characters. As long as we behave in different ways for different audiences and keep secrets from same, we can't expect to keep our balance while we hop from one to another like bunny rabbits running in and out of different burrows.

It's important to see that our social media accounts and walls are an accurate reflection of our minds - we have different 'faces' and 'names' for each account. When we hold multiple accounts, we maintain the fragmentation of our minds and humanity, locking people into the groups we separate them by; for example, family, friends, best friends, work only, drinks pals, ex-boyfriends, people I know, people I don't, or whoever else you can think of - it's a silly game; it wasn't good for me, and I'd venture that it's not good for you. We live in a world - physical and projected - of 'private', 'business', 'social' and 'none of your business' and this will never lead to our peace of mind, or to humanity coming together as One; on the contrary, it creates further separation and therefore, more conflict.

When I consolidated my accounts, it was the first step in my journey to finding the 'true' me. It freed me from a heavy mental burden, freed me from the upkeep of maintaining so many alter-egos and the associated problems that go with that. It was like opening all the doors and windows, allowing the wind to blow away the stale air and dust - carrying with them all my aliases and leaving 'me' behind. Now, I can't get caught out, or feel guilty about a message sent in error to the wrong person - life feels 'above-board' and I know this is the best way for me to be - it's in my best interest. Where it will all take me, I don't know, but I do know that my efforts haven't been in vain.

Louder than a Whisper

*Our hearts are the loveliest landing place
for truths that are hard to face.*

Without sincere self-reflection, we do little to serve the psychological advancement of the Human Race. Instead we serve or function as a human resource, whose only purpose in this world is to advance an antiquated, ritualistic, selfish society, in which we choose to remain ignorant of our true nature; this is a system that abhors benevolence and seeks to complete its own agenda - total control at both ends of the scale. In other words, there are those who want to control and those who don't mind being controlled - you can't have one without the cooperation of the other. We fight, argue, hate, gossip, envy, judge and abuse each other, so much so that we don't recognise that we're doing it; ironically, harming ourselves more than the recipient of our sentiments. We poison rather than nourish our bodies, minds, land, air and water. We harbour guilt, grudges, conditioned negative responses towards others and carry the weight of our pasts on our shoulders, whilst wearing a mask of superiority. We retreat to the safety of our cocoons while pointing the finger of blame with a 'What can I do about it' attitude - mentally assembling jigsaw puzzle pieces that we trim, re-colour or squeeze into place to suit our loves, jealousies or prejudices, for whatever we choose to believe. I find that when I confront anyone with any of the above their kneejerk reaction is 'denial', swiftly followed by the immovable 'I don't want to talk about it' wall. More often than not people respond with 'Why would anyone want to do that?'. Come on! We know that hurting each other is so in our faces that we can't see beyond it. Peace doesn't come out of conflict - only power and submission can come from it and in our hearts we know this - it won't drop out of the sky or come knocking on our front doors either. Some people often repeat 'World War III is coming' messages and this concept really needs to be thought out with something greater than compliant activism. We're always waiting for peace in our world, which means 'war' itself has never actually ended - there's much more to war than guns and bombs. What's it all about? I can't answer that question, but I can think about it, and I do, as living with this level of insanity is unacceptable to me; stepping back a little and seeing the larger picture reveals much. Our world is seriously out of balance and heading towards its own destruction.

Why do we allow it? In my case, I've had to completely change my romantic notions about what a human being is. We can be confrontational, spiteful, violent, aggressive, egotistic, confused, selfish, judgemental, needy, pessimistic and dishonest with ourselves and others, even amongst friends. One of the reasons is because we're frightened. We live in a world of fear exacerbated by the never ending stream of doom-laden negativity; be it war, terror, lies, sickness, suffering and the underlying threat of the destruction of our planet, which pours from the media - 'social' or otherwise. We can't make head nor tail of the information we've been fed and don't know who to trust or what to believe in, if anything at all; we've created a society that's full of doubt, suspicion and judgement - about itself, and that's just the 'news'. Closer to home, we fear the possibility of the content of that 'news' impacting on our own lives; such as, unemployment, loss, violence and poverty. Ultimately, we fear the arrival of our own impending death, or of those who are close to us; we frequently see and feel the pain of loss and mourn those that have 'moved on' ahead of us; the clear message here is that whatever we become attached to we will one day lose, and this makes death dark and undesirable because, death hurts too much and there's nothing we can do about it. I'd suggest that this is one of the reasons we cherish our personal belongings and beliefs so much; when we fear losing something, no matter what it is, we hold onto it that much tighter - it's comforting.

~~~

Language and images are the tools we communicate with and have come to understand; how we interpret them is another matter altogether. Horror, dystopia, science fiction, fantasy, thrillers, adventures and time and space, are just a few of the genres that we love in games, films and books. We find it hard to see these as having any real substance; they're seen as entirely fictional by the majority of people, which makes them hard to conceptualise as anything other than fiction - yet they're worlds that we love to live in. Our inability to ascertain the truth or to know fact from fiction leaves us feeling helpless and vulnerable. We like to see these genres as fictional, because the pain of there being any fact in them is too horrific to contemplate and too complicated to fathom. There's a philosophical thread running through all these entertainments that we don't tend to notice - mostly because we're not looking for it, but we do recognise it. Imagine a nice big fruit cake; the mixture has been thoroughly blended and the cake slowly baked in a hot oven - we can no longer identify the ingredients, save for a few. We love the appearance, taste, texture, aroma and richness of the cake, but rarely consider how it was produced - we're more interested in eating it than anything else. That this cake tastes amazing is the only truth we're interested in; how it was created doesn't interest us past being able to reproduce the product - and many variations of it - in order that we might experience it again … and again.

~~~

Each morning, we wake from a sleep that we either feel rested from, or don't. Our lives are habitual and mundane, regardless of what day of the week it is; weekends are also routine - naturally there are a few variations to this. For many years the first thing I'd do every morning was reach for a cigarette, rush to the kitchen for a cup of coffee and listen to the news. Suitably 'fixed', I had a shower, got dressed, returned to the kitchen for breakfast and then all that invariably followed; work, shopping, meals, commute, television, laundry, social life and sleep again. We perform these routines so often - perfectly timed - usually because our focus is on the next scene; we label our actions a part of 'daily life'. For example, alarm call at 6.00 am, snooze button, alarm again, coffee, shower and dress, kids up, breakfast at 7.00 am; we're always watching the clock and routines demand this - even 'running late' is a routine. Some days these routines are harder to perform - perhaps because we didn't sleep well or went to bed too late, tired, stressed or maybe drunk - making it impossible to 'unwind'. We're unable to re-charge our energy for the following day and therefore, we function less efficiently - something we've come to accept so well that we're unaware of it. Even holidays are routine and often more exhausting than our working lives - they're like moving home, temporarily. Routines are unavoidable to some extent; we need sleep, our meals and at least some form of work/passion to keep us occupied - a raison d'être without which life would have little meaning.

We'd serve humanity much better if we could see that society is our elected master - a master that saps our energy, is self-destructive and at the same time, afraid of its own destruction. There comes a point when the folly of our unsustainable way of life can no longer be ignored, and then we've a choice - start thinking about what we're doing here or continue living with our eyes closed. For me this was a 'no-brainer', and once I took my head out of the sand there was no way I'd ever put it back in again. The whisper was loud and the sound of the bell crystal clear - more than enough to get my attention and make my head ring in confusion. The decision to change does leave us rather disorientated for a while - those bells keep ringing and resonating and that's perfectly normal. When I was very young I'd love to spin round and round until I got giddy and then I'd have to sit for a while until I recovered my senses - it's confusing for our brains/minds. This is rather what it can feel like to retire or to be made redundant; the pressure of work is suddenly off and, unless we're one of the super-planners, we can be at a loss for anything interesting or stimulating to do, unless we've already found our passion and purpose, in which case we're more than happy to have more time to pursue it. We get confused when we break cherished habits whether we enjoy them or not; any habit is an addiction and therefore, hard to break.

When we begin to question everything the fog begins to lift and things become clearer - not crystal clear, because what we see is so unfamiliar. It takes time to clear the clouds of conditioning and to change our point of view. Think of it as walking without knowing where we're going; there's no GPS, map, road signs or compass; however, despite being unclear about our destination, something keeps us going. The drive is powerful and our energy increases with each step. It's not that we didn't have this energy before, but rather that we expended it elsewhere. Energy is like money; if we waste it on useless things we've nothing left for the things we really need; however, our own energy is more valuable than money can ever be, but we can't know this until we start preserving it. If you're struggling with the concept of money being energy then just change perspective a little - think about how much power it has in our world.

The road mentioned above probably seems a bit silly and I can see that. Why would anyone want to think about walking along a metaphorical road that may lead nowhere? I can't tell you where it goes, but think about this - where does the road you're on now lead to?

The answer to the latter question is known by everyone - absolutely nowhere unless you consider the graveyard to be your only option for a choice of destination. This alone - illusion or not - was enough for me to change direction; there's not much point in continuing along the road if it's not heading where we want to go and when we realise this, our fear of changing dissolves along with our will to continue on the same path. Okay, so we might not know where we want to go, but that's not important at this stage; what is important is that we know where we don't want to go. Yes, our bodies still end up in the graveyard and if we believe this 'material' world is all there is then that's rather discouraging; however, material is not all there is and despite the beliefs of some people, 'something' else does exist and I'd suggest that's worth thinking about - we know it very well.

~~~

In this world - as we understand it - we have to live with 'time' and telling you that it doesn't exist would generally be unacceptable; it was to me for a long time (no pun intended). More often than not this idea leaves us feeling inadequate and frustrated because we may not understand it straight away - please don't give up on it. We've had time in our lives since our 'births' and we're reluctant to let it go - the mind and ego want to hold onto it and they're powerful, influential and unyielding. Society reinforces the illusion of time by putting clocks and watches just about everywhere we turn. It's almost impossible not to know what time it is or what we should be doing at any particular time; for example, working hours, tea breaks, lunch breaks and holidays; 'life' is always 'arriving' and 'leaving' via various timetables whilst we plod on. On this 'journey', some days feel good and can leave us feeling as though we're floating on air, but some feel bad - the bad can drag on for weeks, months or even years. Nothing really changes other than how we cope with day-to-day problems as they present themselves; however, this is a necessary part of our journey and therefore, not wasted. It's only wasted if we don't keep moving and what doesn't move is effectively, dead.

~~~

We live in a dualistic world of all possibility and that means we can turn it all around; one way to do this is to observe our own behaviour and change it according to how we want our world to be, as discussed in 'Observation'. We need each other and we're all a part of a greater whole. All of the above traits I mentioned regarding humanity can be changed - we need only make the choice and the process begins. Yes, yes and yes, it's hard and feels contradictory, but our lives are hard and contradictory anyway - as is to be expected in a dualistic world. One of the wonderful things about dualism is that we have choices; there's a 'yes' and a 'no', a 'this' and a 'that'. All we have to do is choose to change and when we make this choice something different evolves, but not if our decision isn't in earnest. If we change, we'll find that there's so much more to us; for a start, that the Human Race is One, life is worthwhile and wisdom, grace and humility are worth striving for. Our focus needs to be on, not what others are doing, but on what we're doing. We need to make a decision to be done with pain and suffering (my continuous affirmation) and mean it. We've everything to gain and absolutely nothing to lose. When we see this, the layers of beliefs we've created for our 'characters' fall away and that's very revealing. There'd be little point in just looking at a box covered in wrapping paper and ribbons - we'd never find out what was inside if we didn't remove them. Life demands something from us, but we continue to ignore this and instead, we take more and more from it - returning to its river only our anger, tears, refuse and frustrations.

We make decisions to change our lives all the time; for example, when we:

- Go on a diet.
- Make a new year's resolution.
- Start a new hobby.
- Decide to get fit.
- Move house.
- Begin writing a book.
- Join a group.

But these days, in most cases, they're only temporary pastimes or more accurately, passing fads. These occupations make us feel great at first, but they soon get pushed to one side when we get bored with them, or find something else to fill our lives with - our homes and garages are full of unfinished projects. I see these fads as being rather like fireworks - they look impressive in that first skyward rush that explode into enthusiasm, but they soon lose their sparkle and then, the burnt stick of 'reality' falls back to the ground. We can easily mistake these fads for our true passion, but passion doesn't burn away or fizzle out. Passion is the fuel - it drives itself and once ignited, it can't be easily extinguished.

The closest physical and psychological relationship we can ever have is with ourselves - from birth to death. We can never leave this 'home'- not even for a second. This is so important to contemplate. Problems have arisen because we believe we're the person in the mirror, the personality we created, the slob, the professional, the big man, the small man, the characters in films, the beauty or the beast. Our pasts define us; for example, I am who I am because of my past and therefore can't let go of it - this is just an excuse not to remove its stubborn stain. These beliefs are like the tethers of a hot air balloon preventing it from going on its adventures - until the stakes are pulled out, the balloon isn't going anywhere.

I know of some people who work well past their retirement age, perhaps because they're terrified they won't know what to do with their time or have enough money to survive on; however, once the chord is cut, most people wonder why they didn't do it earlier. The real terror here is that when we retire there's nothing left in our lives that defines us, so we refer to ourselves as what we used to be; I was a doctor, a secretary, an engineer etc., and these tend to be what we like to talk about with other people in later life - reliving our past glories. It's important to see that these professions aren't who we are - they're what we do. We allow society to define us with its various labels and divisions; such as, unemployed, professional, white collar, labourer, academic, elite or lower class, to name but a few. We have no boundaries, unless we choose to construct them, or allow others to forge them for us. When we were young children we had very little control over this situation, but now we do. Yes, it's true that we are where/who we think we are because of our past, and when we realise this we have the opportunity to break free from its grip. Why do I say 'opportunity'; wouldn't we just 'break free'? No! When push comes to shove, and the enormity of what stands before us becomes apparent, fear kicks in; we then start to backtrack and make excuses about why we can't change; excuses that allow our past to hold us in its comforting arms, until the 'right moment', the 'right tool' or the 'right person' comes along - safe in the knowledge that they never will.

Betrayal

No-one can let you down, unless you depend on them.

Unlike the rest of the chapters in this book, I was asked to write about the subject of betrayal. I skimmed this topic a little in 'Completeness', but here I want to focus more on betrayal itself. This request was the first I ever received and for a while I felt reluctant to write it because I saw it as a part of someone else's journey and therefore, it didn't belong in my book. However, on reflection, the topic came into my field of vision for a reason so I decided to examine it and now, it fits rather nicely right here. Often, the things we put up the most resistance to are *exactly* what we need to focus on.

My initial thoughts about betrayal were to do with disloyalty, particularly with regard to personal - non-familial - relationships, because this request was put to me in that context. However, like all things, when we zoom in closer to any topic - not relying on conditioning for explanations - a new and clear understanding of it evolves. Betrayal is probably one of the most destructive actions one human being can do to another, or to themselves. It's 'breaching an agreement' and we're betrayed every day in one way or another by:

- A stark contrast between an image on a packet and its contents.

- Things promised, but never received.
- The betrayal of confidences.
- Political manifestos that don't deliver.
- The infidelity of a trusted friend.
- Ourselves for 'believing' in things we *know* to be false.

and much, much more. With this new understanding comes simplification and responsibility. When we hold onto the aches and pains of betrayal, simplification and responsibility are the last things we want to hear about - we prefer to hold others accountable.

More often than not we already know who's going to betray us well in advance - we prefer to gloss over the indications that we first noticed. Some of the things I once found endearing in other people proved to be 'early warning signs' that I chose to ignore; one example of this was the alcohol habit of one of the men I married - his drinking began several hours before lunch and ended at bedtime. At first he didn't drink too much, but it quickly became apparent that his consumption of alcohol had been reduced/hidden in order to 'secure' our relationship. Other examples of advanced warnings of betrayal are a 'roving eye', flirtatious personality and various excuses we somehow *know* are lies. We've been taught that no-one is perfect and therefore, we don't expect perfection; we're happy to accept a person's 'down-sides' and can initially convince ourselves that these are 'charming' - because we *want* them to be. If we think back far enough to the beginning of these relationships, we realise, in many cases, that what we now call 'betrayal' was, on discovery, anything but a surprise. Still, we feel 'let down', again and again.

~~~

It's impossible to talk about betrayal without talking about trust. Trust is something that grows, rather like the construction of a spider's web and gradually its delicate threads build up into this beautiful thing we call trust. However, if that web gets damaged by the touch of betrayal, we can never restore it to its original form - try as we may, we'll always be aware of those broken threads - giving rise to suspicion and the expectation of further betrayal. Suspicion (mistrust) is something that increasingly pervades our society in all walks of life; business, private, social and personal - so much so that we don't even trust *ourselves* and therefore, faithfully rely on the authority and consequently, the guidance of others. A great many people are reluctant to reveal their identity online and I've had many refuse my offer to send them free copies of my books - some didn't want to reveal their addresses. Even when the intention is kindness, people feel threatened in some way and find it difficult, if not impossible, to trust each other - often the result of many stories in our various forms of media that focus on betrayal, violence and other negativity.

These stories include the shattering of an illusion; for example, in someone famous we once trusted - our apparent 'fallen heroes'. We can't trust the stories and because suspicion has been planted into our minds, we no longer trust the person concerned regardless of whether or not they're innocent; suspicion and judgement are powerful condemners - with or without proof. More importantly, we believed in these people and what they stood for - we 'loved' them - and it *seems* as though our trust in that was broken; repeated stories like this leave us unable to trust or believe in anything at all. Because of this we're more likely to accept the authority of those 'in control' in our world - they so often remind us 'never to give out our personal details' and to 'check the credentials' of just about everyone we come into contact with. The 'authorities' offer us a protective parental arm to snuggle into; to accept and rely on this 'snuggle' could be unwise.

In this mixed up world it has become necessary to double or triple lock our doors and windows and in many cases, to live in 'secure' blocks that have more than a hint of penitentiary about them. Security is a highly profitable business which translated means, that the creation of communities that live in fear is profitable. Despite so much betrayal and suspicion in our world we *still* tend to jump straight into new relationships or one night stands and in some cases believe that this makes us 'free-spirited'. What it really does is misleadingly make us feel as though we're in control of our lives - it injects a little artificial and temporary *freshness* into them, but on a deeper level, these relationships confirm what we believe - that we're 'not good enough' - and leave us feeling more insecure; mostly, they don't contain anything worth holding onto and we know it.

Misplaced trust is like a walking stick we believed could stand our weight and one day, while we're leaning on it, it breaks and we injure ourselves falling down. We can repair the stick with glue or tape it together, but we'll never be able to trust it to support our weight again. Trust is something we give to someone else and when they betray it, it can hurt more than we've ever been hurt before, leaving a deep, ugly and *unforgettable* scar. To give someone our complete trust is to invite them to betray us one day - it also means we rely on them to treasure that trust as much as *we* think they should. A broken trust is the shattering of a firm expectation - with full confidence - that we can rely on someone or something outside of ourselves. The problem with this expectation is that it doesn't allow for the fact that we're all fundamentally the same and - save for our different experiences - destined to experience the same 'ending'. The walking stick we leaned on broke because it was flawed in some way, and though we suspected as much, we still chose to put our trust in it; whatever we entrust to another human being or organisation, we run the risk of losing one day.

The betrayals mentioned in the above list come about because we live in a fragmented world. We're divided (and sub-divided) from each other in hundreds of ways and therefore, as individuals, we reach out to others for what we believe we lack. We reach out because we feel incomplete and we feel this because we *are* incomplete. There's a thought that lives in the back of our mind 'There's more to me than this - I'm missing something important', but every time it pops up we push it right back where it came from; it's called a *Hintergedanke* in German, which means a 'nagging unconscious thought', but we don't trust it. To ignore it isn't very different than refusing to open the mail that's delivered into our letterboxes. One person I know told me there's no point in changing the way he lives, because no-one else will, and this is just one reason why the insanity of this world persists; this idea also demonstrates how we prefer to place ourselves in what we think of as 'safety in numbers' situations. Trusting ourselves - and our instincts - involves sacrifice and determination. More importantly, it involves a lot of self-reflection - not one of our favourite pastimes, and so we keep ourselves busy in order to avoid it. When we question everything, then by definition it follows that we must leave everything we believed in behind, including our suffering, pain, mistakes and regrets. This process includes all forms of 'security' in our relationships with others and yes, that includes family; relationship implies attachment and with that attachment, we run the risk of betrayal; the greater the attachment, the greater the injury we sustain when the walking stick breaks. No, I'm *not* saying anyone has to leave their home or their family; all that's needed is to examine the subject, observe the world we live in, how we interact with it, and deal with whatever follows those actions.

~~~

The betrayal of a child is caused by the same fragmentation of society. For a long time, I hated my father for putting me into an orphanage, particularly at such a young and tender age. I was unable to protest or defend myself against the staff and saw the world as an unfair place to live in. I was unable to complain to anyone or report incidents, as I never had the language or knowledge that it was possible to protest against mistreatment - for me, it was both terrifying and normal and more than likely the reason I decided to forget about it (most of it anyway). I felt wretched in the orphanage - as though I were something worthless that had been discarded. I now see this differently. We can't expect our parents, whose lives have been as painful and problematic as our own, to be loving towards us; they simply don't know how. This new understanding doesn't make what happened okay, but it does help to see how a particular situation came about and more importantly, how not to dwell on it. We tend to be pretty bad parents to our children; we give them 'too little' or 'too much', tell them scary stories, threaten them if they don't 'behave' themselves, and after they reach school age have very little to do with their upbringing.

When they begin school, we lose whatever influence we once had over them - it passes into the hands of our various forms of education and media, who are people just like us. I've already had feedback from a friend on my 'bad parents' comment, so I'll elaborate a little. Are we looking after the planet and eradicating violence for our children or future generations? No, we continue to destroy it - and ourselves - in many different ways. This is also a form of betrayal; we're damaging and poisoning the world our children must live in and making them afraid - very afraid.

~~~

Let's get back to that stick for a moment. Sometimes the stick breaks because it was leant on too heavily. Too much trust can be a heavy burden for another person to carry and I'd suggest that this trust can be broken, not always with the intention of hurting another person, but because the weight is too much to bear. The trust of billions of people is in the hands of an untrustworthy minority who head political, religious and financial organisations. This gives them enormous power - *our* power - and we don't even know who they are, yet rely on them to sort out the mess our world is in. It's *us* who need to take care of our own welfare; we're the light *and* the shadow in this world and therefore, accountable for our own predicament. Any way you look at it, giving trust and risking betrayal of that trust are the prices we have to pay for relying on something or someone else. Trusting in someone else leaves us vulnerable and that means powerless and in fear. We prefer to walk through a 'minefield' after someone else has 'cleared the path' ahead - then we'll be more than happy to join them. There's nothing to be learnt from following in someone else's footsteps; they can't clear *our* path for us because they haven't lived through our experiences. Because most people want to live a risk free existence, nothing changes. Most importantly, our reluctance to change is one of the greatest betrayals of all - the betrayal of ourselves and consequently, of humanity - it's also 'spiritual laziness'.

The Abyss of Loneliness

Loneliness is what happens when the connection between ourselves and our source is broken.

As a child, I can't remember exactly at what age, but it was over a period of many years, I used to watch one of my sisters closely. I saw her as a role model, because she was the only relative around at the time; in some ways, I saw her as a surrogate mother though I know that was the furthest thing from her mind. I'd try to dress like her, mimic her walk, talk and copy some of her other well-rehearsed traits, but these attempts to 'become' her only left me feeling more confused than ever about my place in the world. I depended on her for my happiness and wanted to share her friends, because I never had any of my own; this always backfired and I don't think I meant any more to her than a pat-on-the-head 'little sister' - an act that made her feel good about herself and left me feeling betrayed and humiliated on many occasions. I was a means to an end, as was she. I'd allow her to choose my clothes as I'd no idea what would or wouldn't suit me and she looked good in anything. My sister always chose something unflattering for me, knowing that I'd wear whatever she suggested. The nearest I can get to explaining how I felt at the time is to say that I'd been born on the wrong planet, into the wrong body, to the wrong parents and had the wrong siblings; I was effectively, lost.

This sister, in later years had many 'friends' and a busy social life. I was invited to go out with her, but I was still introduced to her friends as 'my little sister' and ended up feeling alone at parties, pubs, or bars; they held only more emptiness for me because no matter how hard I tried, I was unable to fit in - for the life of me I couldn't see the attraction. Years later, I realised we'd been looking for the same thing (acceptance) and - ironically - she'd wanted to be as much like me as I'd wanted to be like her, which came as rather a shock when I first realised it. We both needed to 'belong' somewhere and to be 'loved'. Despite her popularity, she was as unhappy and lonely as me; the parties, alcohol, drugs and crowds only served to numb the pain of her loneliness.

~~~

My perspective on loneliness has changed over the years and I now see that loneliness is not the same as being alone. Loneliness is a deep longing for completeness, which we search for in companionship, friendship and our need to relate to someone on the same level as ourselves, which is why we need to go out socialising and the like. 'Alone' doesn't need any of society's attractions and is free from the struggle of trying to 'fit in'. What was really happening inside my head was a resistance to partying my life away - counting down the minutes to an 'acceptable' time to go home, yet dreading the same loneliness that drove me to the party in the first place. However, the happiness we seek *can't* be found in this way - it's like trying to draw water from a well with no bucket on the end of our rope. It's important to see that just about everyone is doing the same thing from an innate longing to 'connect'. This need can't be met by anyone or anything else, because the only 'agenda' at these social events is to curb the loneliness that lies in our hearts. I needed something that held deeper meaning and in later years this led me to challenge what I'd come to know as 'reality'. It wasn't that I was unable to express myself, but rather that my expression was met with indifference; yet I kept on trying and failing, which increased my feelings of inadequacy - leaving me feeling lonelier than ever. It's easy in our loneliness to try to find happiness on the 'outside' through social activities, because this is how we've been taught to do it through clubs, groups, teams, classes and of course our parents and siblings.

Loneliness causes us to hide - from ourselves and others - behind self-constructed barriers and it's terrifying to think about taking them down. The power of our loneliness is much greater than our ability to overcome it and hits us hard from every angle (inside and out). No matter where we go, what we do or how busy we keep ourselves there's no way to escape our loneliness other than to seek out its cause. I mentioned to a friend that I was writing this chapter and when I asked what loneliness meant to her she replied 'I don't like to think about loneliness, because it makes me feel so lonely'. Another friend said 'You can have a huge family and lots of friends, but behind closed doors you feel lonely, because it's always you that makes the effort

- which is upsetting - so you create a distance between you and *them* which results in you feeling lonelier still'. For my part, I started writing this chapter many times, because I was both drawn to and repelled by it - I also procrastinated. In all three cases, it's clear to me that loneliness is something we struggle to understand, face, live with or talk about and for this reason, I've written this chapter.

~~~

In general, we tend to consider anyone who's lonely to be socially *unacceptable*. The lonely feel that there's something wrong with them, because they're unable to play 'the game' *correctly*. They're labelled as 'loners', 'misfits' or given some other belittling title. In truth, the lonely would like to connect with people, but in a way that's more meaningful than having a 'good time', fitting in with a crowd, discussing the latest bad news or following a particular fashion; the lonely resist these 'guided' definitions of themselves. 'Loners' are *deep* and I'd suggest that it's for this reason most people choose to stay away from them - 'deep' is not our idea of 'fun'. People who are lonely see possibility; they see the beauty in how we *could* live, rather than how we do. Somehow, the lonely know true friendship, but are unable to find it and tend to hate themselves far more than they think others do. The more we see that isn't good in our society, the more space we put between ourselves and those who choose not to. The trouble with things like parties, is that they're someone else's idea of fun (the host); we're expected to fit in, and all there really is to do at them is listen to the problems people want to tell us about, feel frustrated that no one wants to listen to ours, discuss current affairs, behave badly, eat party food, compete with each other or drink alcohol - formulaic and meaningless activities. These social gatherings are often a distraction from the pain of reality, memories we'd prefer to forget and an uncertain future - a temporary escape from the mind for everyone who 'succeeds' at enjoying them. We put each other under pressure to *develop* fashionable social skills and appearances, which are nothing more than prescribed antidotes for loneliness and we do this in order for humanity to fulfil a need for company and 'excitement'. Popularity is something that's subjective and superficial; it's abstract and requires someone to be admired and, a trail of admirers; all of whom must play out their roles until the party comes to an end, which ultimately it must do. One modern example of this scenario is the plague of 'selfies' that has hit social media websites - selfies that scream out 'Look at me!' Where is the wisdom in this sort of lifestyle; is wisdom something society intends to eradicate?

The lonely know something's missing from their lives *and* also from the lives of others who suffer the consequences of our 'partying', and demands for more toys and excitement - they find gatherings painful, rather than enjoyable. No-one sees or hears us screaming; we're effectively invisible, and that leaves us with a deep and inexplicable feeling of 'out of placeness' or if you will, an inability to be comfortable with our surroundings despite the fact that we can't go anywhere else. We don't so easily escape the knowledge that so many in the world are suffering on our behalf and we can't live with the weight of that on our shoulders. We're left staring at a reflection that we don't want to look at - let alone think about - and consequently, keep ourselves busy in order to keep our gaze averted.

We vacillate between our loneliness and the pull of the world of 'excitement' and social gatherings in the hope that they might bring an end to it; for example, if we happen to meet Mr or Mrs Right or a new 'best friend'. We're not at all comfortable in this 'ping pong' situation because deep down all we really want is a permanent end to our loneliness, rather than a respite from it. We're the frontier between the two worlds; as the mind sharpens, it's possible to see that this frontier doesn't actually exist. It's not possible to see this clearly until we're prepared to remove our walls altogether, which leaves us vulnerable, but how else will we ever be able to see the 'whole' picture. Deep down we all want the same thing - inner peace and happiness.

Aside from when we're feeling lonely at home, it's not just at parties that we feel this loneliness, but also at school, work or in any other place where human beings are gathered together, regardless of their age. Just take a look around a crowded train or bus next time you're on one - no-one speaks to anyone else, but rather they're absorbed in their own worlds. The deepest feelings of loneliness aren't just felt when we're alone, but so often in public places where we want to reach out to others but our arms aren't long enough - or strong enough - to break down their resistance. I'll go so far as to say that this includes at 'spiritual' meetings; most people have only their own agenda, and if we say something that contradicts what they *want* to hear, conflict follows and more barriers are raised instead of removing existing ones. Mostly - deep down - we're thinking 'I don't want to listen to *you*, I want you to listen to *me*' - often we're not listening to what the other person is saying and waiting to cut in to the conversation with our 'take' on things. These gatherings can leave us feeling that no-one knows or understands us. However, we can take consolation from knowing that they don't know or understand themselves either.

~~~

Perhaps it's our fear of loneliness that's created so many homes for the elderly - before they'd remain with their families but now more and more of us have our *own* lives to live and can't handle the responsibility for others. It's possible that we see our elderly family members as being lonelier and more isolated than we're willing to imagine, or live with. Society takes up all of our waking time and therefore, we don't even *begin* to reflect on these important matters until we close our eyes, but by then we're invariably so tired that we fall asleep. Where can this situation end though; if our children become too difficult to handle will we, in the future, also think about giving them up to some other authority? It's already necessary in many families that children are cared for by childminders so this isn't such an alien concept for the future - it's been woven into literature for a long time now. From who or where will these children ever gain their wisdom?

Loneliness can cause us to feel as though no-one knows or cares that we're here. Some of the deepest forms of loneliness we can experience are; for example, when we've been out all day and despite crowds, not managed to speak to another soul, or when we're checking to see if our telephone is broken because no-one has called. Other examples are when we:

- Watch the clock to see if it's time to go to bed.
- Pass our time *staying* in bed.
- Make a cup of tea before the last one we made gets cold.
- Flick through television channels and never really watching anything.
- Nip out to the local shop for something we don't need, just because we want to see another face.
- Check for messages when we know full well there aren't any.

- Feel as though we're the only person in the world.
- Comfort eat, drink alcohol or take drugs.
- Look to others for our security.

There are some people I know of who are so desperate to connect that they read, and reply to, their spam as though it were from a friend; this is a dreadful state of affairs for humanity to find itself in and no-one should have to suffer like that. There isn't a human being who can make us feel better in these situations; we lock people out because they don't understand us, and ourselves in because *we* don't understand them. However, all of us want to be seen and heard by somebody else and because we want the same thing, we can't find it. In other words, we can't hear the cries of others while we're crying out to be heard. Interestingly, when I was feeling lonely I never thought about or noticed anyone else that felt the same way; this is how deeply loneliness penetrates - we can't see further than our own agony. No matter how awful loneliness feels, it doesn't have to be that way; we can find all we need within and now I see that my loneliness was in fact a blessing. For many years I didn't use the time wisely, or realise that I was my own greatest friend.

In all the loneliness situations I've mentioned above, the barriers we put up serve to prevent honest communication. The conflict is both external and internal and has a deeper meaning than is at first apparent - it ignores the innate *need* that I mentioned earlier, to connect with each other, not only on a physical level, but on a psychological one as well. Understanding this is pivotal if we ever want to bring an end to conflict. Serving one 'side' can't bring any balance into our lives, but only more struggle - isn't that what happens in war? Each side fighting each other and each person fighting their own internal battle, and from that we kid ourselves that we can bring about peace. As mentioned above, the walls of both worlds (internal and external) must be removed, or else it isn't possible to see what's actually going on. The apples of one tree are its fruits and there's no conflict between them or the tree that bore them - that would be ridiculous. Likewise, we're all the fruits of humanity and it's equally ridiculous to think that we're not, *or* that one of us is more important than another. We're One and unlike the apples, we're not only physical, but conscious, and therefore have a great deal more responsibility in our world than we're prepared to - or do - take on. Like the apples we have an origin - connecting to it when we're feeling lonely is the best and wisest thing we can ever do. We feel lonely because we're disconnected from our source and resist reconnection - for whatever reason. This causes us to seek solace in the company of others, who are as lonely as we are and therefore, cannot help us. When we figure this out and reconnect to our origin - by deconstructing our barriers and examining how they were erected - we'll better see what's magic and permanent - what never has and never will change.

Personality, Pride & Other Tough Stuff

Pride is the pedestal we climb up onto
- shame and humiliation, what we feel
when we fall from it.

To understand what pride is, we need to know what it is we're proud of and how we came to be proud of it. In furtherance of this, it's necessary to put together some of the things I've previously discussed, and to examine how they relate to us personally. If we want to strip ourselves of our illusions, we must first understand how they've been woven together over the course of our lives and how we became so attached to them and to other people; we can't see the truth while we still believe the deception. It's a process of 'unpicking' the weave and we resist because we don't *want* to be unpicked, but these traits were not with us when we were born and are not part of our true nature. We're possessive and protective of our identities, convictions and contradictions - though we tend to be dissatisfied with how we see ourselves. We find a sort of comfortable security in our attachments to the familiar - rather like a child holding on to a torn and ragged favourite teddy bear that no other 'teddy' can replace. Our creations are our 'pride and joy'; who, after all, would we be without them?

Human beings are the most cunning of creatures and skilful at assembling character traits and appearances that are nothing more than a metaphysical photofit of what we call 'ourselves'. These traits make up our character/personality and we continually tweak them for any given situation, wearing them proudly as though they were works of art - for works of art they are. We pretend, in the main, to be interested in others by calling ourselves generous, hospitable, kind, charitable, respectable, compassionate and approachable, but usually we're nothing of the sort - how could we be when we live in such a mischievous world that's obsessed with 'self'. Generosity for example, can't exist without a need for it and surely for us to behave kindly towards someone, implies unkindness in the first place; we're full of contradictions. One business example of this is a answerphone greeting that the creator probably thinks is funny 'Your call is important to us … please hold the line'; the call can't be important at all as often, some thirty minutes or so later we're still holding on - so they get away with it. If we all hang up immediately after hearing the message the companies would see how important our call actually is, and would have to adapt their system to become one that values rather than wastes the time of its clients. We're master imposters and pranksters trying to con and outwit each other with just about every breath we take and we're only interested in - on a conscious level - what's going on inside our particular 'bubble'.

The concept that our personalities are woven can be a difficult one to grasp. We tend to see ourselves as being entirely physical, ignoring - or having no curiosity about - our spiritual nature - we think in 'ego' mode. We take great pride in our 'creations' and nurture them until we become exactly what we want to be; professional, social, downright miserable or whatever else we choose to make of our lives. More threads are interwoven over the course of time; for example, at the age of five, we've no idea about things like romance or how we'll relate to it when we're older. We do however, begin to formulate this trait through fairy tales and other stories building up our dreams of what it would be like to be 'grown up'; for example, how we'll interact with the different people who cross our path. We wrap ourselves up in these 'dreams' and if anyone attempts to expose them, we move into 'defence mode' to keep the fabric of our *imagined* world intact.

The difference in our reaction when we see the innocence, beauty and the miracle of a new born baby and an adult is stark. The adult was once the baby who has grown into everything we've added on to it over the years including jealousy, hatred, judgement, opinions, fear and pride; however, the innocence, beauty and the miracle are no longer recognisable to us behind our hardened hearts. As a baby our character begins to be formed according to our environment; everything we see, do, taste, touch, smell, hear and everyone we meet influences and shapes our personality - society is our 'parent'. Society is the mould that shaped our characters; we hold on to the accumulated memories that parented us, because we'd be unrecognisable to ourselves without them. We however, add to our 'egos' with every thought, gradually building up so many layers that even *we* can't see through them. We get caught up in the illusion and change - where possible - our appearances to fit (metaphysically and physically); I'll be a brunette, a missionary, or a judge for example. We tweak what we see as our faults through 'new year's resolutions' or 'fads', but these rarely amount to any change, because they tend to have no more meaning than a change of clothes. On a deep level we don't like who we become, but as our 'personality' is 'apparently' all there is to us, we hold on to it tightly in order to survive; our inner character is very different to our projected one which to all intents and purposes, is the shield that protects - or hides - our true nature - the two are in conflict.

One of the features of living in a dualistic world are the contradictions present in each of us - these are the internal arguments we can't get any peace from. Rather than living in a way that prolongs our lives making them happier and healthier, we generally live by a 'death wish', and in order to make this wish come true we poison our minds, water, land, air and bodies. Despite increasing laws on 'Health and Safety' there's little evidence that we care about them, until we're personally affected; for example, when we - or someone close to us - becomes ill or has an accident, or perhaps if dirty water comes out of our kitchen taps. How can we have so many concerns about health and safety on the one hand and cause so much devastation and illness with the other? We know the risks and damage caused by smoking and alcohol for example, yet corporations make enormous profits from them; we're paying for our own destruction in the name of a 'good time'. We rush to support charities during a crisis, but generally, make no effort to eradicate the need for them. Far too often we prefer things just the way they are - things that are bad for us, as opposed to good; we become addicted to them as we turn to them for 'comfort', which is really 'escape'. If you don't agree that we like the 'bad' just take a look at any given week of yours regarding; food (unnatural), cleaning the house (chemicals), television, newspapers, fuel consumption, gossip, waste, judgement, thoughts, spending, smoking, alcohol, mind dramas and pride. We can't be perfect in this world, but we can become aware and that in itself will make a huge difference, which we can't see or benefit from, until we earnestly put our minds to it. The only possible reason I can think of for humanity to live this way is that we all know, deep down, that our true nature is infinite, so we play for high stakes believing that there really isn't any risk at all. Does this argument have any substance? Only we can decide that, as individuals - not in groups.

~~~

Pride is an inflated sense of achievement and superiority that allows us to hold our heads up so high that we can't - and don't want to - see where we're going. We award it to ourselves in the form of self-congratulation, while bathing in our pool of glory and achievement. Society encourages us to take these 'bows' with a host of awards and certificates that we aim for in one way or another, because with them we become 'successful' and are considered to be 'upright citizens'; in other words, we get the approval and respect of the 'authorities' that set *their* standards for us to achieve. One of the most serious side effects of this ballooning of our egos is that it leaves others far behind in our wake of gratification - causing division and resentment. Another effect is that we become what others want us to be (copies of our predecessors) and can therefore, never discover who we really are. I mentioned in an earlier chapter - 'Am I Good Enough' - that there were three things we can do from the top of a ladder; stay there, climb down or fall off it and 'staying there' has surely got to be the least stimulating of options and because of this boredom, the most dangerous. We need things to do, see or think about - things that are exciting, new and challenging, no matter how meaningless they may appear to be.

The mind needs continuous action and it doesn't want to be quiet even for a moment; a so-called 'couch potato' is still stimulating his mind by watching the television - or rather having it stimulated for him - regardless of what he's watching or how many times the program has been shown before - repetition is not boring for the mind and our lives are full of it. Our mind seeks stimulation anywhere it can get it and this, I'd suggest, is why we keep ourselves so 'occupied'. Television, radio, newspapers, commuting, work, shopping, chores and our social lives feed the mind's need to feel all sorts of emotions like fear, sadness, happiness, despair, frustration and anger; our world has become so noisy that what we can't bear - more than anything else - is silence. Whatever we do with our daily lives - regardless of where we are on the 'ladder' - we strive for more and more and *more* of it, but the stimulation comes from something external and therefore, it's nothing to do with self-discovery and, nothing new.

It's possible to watch our pride in action - it's one of our ego's treasured facets. The ego is the star of our 'show' and it doesn't want to leave the stage even for a moment. The mind is always scheming to maintain and increase its hold on us and it's highly efficient and very much 'on the ball' - it's as sharp and as dangerous as a dagger. Pride comes into being when we identify ourselves with our 'achievements' or in some cases, achievements we claim to have made, and also when we polish our appearance/character - rather like shining up those medals. But pride isn't just about medals and ladder rungs - it's the sharpest tool that separates us from our true nature and from others. Pride is:

- Apparently, the number one sin.
- The need to win an argument - though we may not know what we're talking about - and also to shout louder than our 'opponent' in an attempt to intimidate them into submission.

- A refusal to pick up the phone when we want to speak to someone, but are unable to bring ourselves to dial their number.
- Boasting.
- Refusing good advice because *we* know 'better'.
- The belief that we deserve the respect and admiration of others.
- A control mechanism.
- All about 'Me'.
- The wall that refuses to ask for help when we need it.
- The refusal of help that's being offered.

First we have to come clean about our world and then we'll be able to take responsibility for all that's going on in it. Our intention in these cases is to stand our ground - no matter what - even when there's no solid ground to stand on; pride prevents us from retreating or admitting error. We know full well when we're doing this, but refuse to back down; watching our pride in action brings that to an end because just in watching it, we become more self-aware and also see how ridiculous pride actually is. If you wish to see what pride means to the collective mind just do an internet search for the word and see what comes up both on the *web* tab and on *images* - you may be surprised at the results - they are there because *we* put them there. As our awareness increases it becomes very difficult to maintain the façade and increasingly, we're able to admit 'error' without feeling humiliated and with this change our pride begins to subside. Before blaming society for being a 'bad' parent to us, we must first ask ourselves if we've been 'good' children in it.

~~~

Society is an accurate reflection of the human mind; proud, stoic and resistant to change - though we collectively agree to live in it and to uphold its practises and regimes. It's what we do every day, and each one of us is, and has been, put through an educational system that demands the continuation of this proud society - it's a generational loop and it's an unhealthy and unworthy one. Despite society being unhealthy and destructive we're proud to be a part of it - flying our particular flags. We tend not to want society changed or criticised, particularly by those who think differently, seemingly posing a threat to the *status quo*, which we fight to maintain - a *status quo* that's created a 'hive mind' mentality. The world is the way it is because the majority of people like it this way, despite their protestations to the contrary. It's important to discern that we can't find our *centre* when our 'walls of pride' are up or when we're following somebody else's directions, because we're relying on an unhealthy system and an unhealthy mind to do it for us - which they're incapable of doing.

When our pride takes a 'hit', a wave of mixed emotions washes over us - ranging from anger to fear. Our pride gets hit when someone thinks they could've done something better than us -effectively deprecating our efforts. We don't like criticism, regardless of whether it's constructive or not. We see what we do as excellent - even if only by effort - because we've rehearsed it for a long time and to have someone not see us as we want them to, hurts our pride very much. One example of this is when we invite friends to dinner and one of them comments - across the table - that we added too much salt to the meal, or that they'd let us have their perfected recipe for what we spent all day preparing. Pride is wobbly and easily offended, particularly when it's met with such condescension. I'm sure that every one of us knows that feeling of vulnerability; such as, when we trip over a paving slab and everyone who saw it watches as our face reddens and we struggle to get up again - believing, if not knowing, that all eyes are upon us. This is also how it feels when attention is unfavourably drawn to us in the company of others, such as with my 'pat-on-the-head' big sister in the previous chapter.

Men feel vulnerable if they leave their trousers undone and women if they're caught with their skirt tucked into their knickers as they come out of the public toilets, particularly if someone points it out before they realise it. In these moments of discomposure, we feel humiliated and exposed because one of our walls collapsed in a momentary lapse of concentration - we dropped our guard and our ego *never* likes that. Two of the layers behind our pride are 'shame' and 'embarrassment' and we feel these when our wall of pride shows cracks, leaving us exposed because of our 'failure' - usually a failure to keep up expected appearances. Imagine, if you will, an actor whose moustache slips or forgets his lines in the middle of his finest performance - he's no longer fully 'under cover' and shows his infallibility, as he struggles to straighten the moustache or to remember his lines - in front of everyone. Even if we correct the error before anyone notices we worry that someone *might* have seen us because we're so self-conscious about the things we do. In the reverse of this situation we get to keep our wall up when we watch the misfortunes of others, and I'd add that we're happy these didn't happen to us. If something unfortunate happens to someone we dislike or disapprove of, then we may get a certain amount of enjoyment from the incident and consider that justice has been done - a rather judgemental and superior attitude to take, but we take this stance often and state that 'it served them right', or if we don't know them we may think that they 'must have deserved it'; bad is okay as long as it's happening to someone else, and unfortunately this attitude has reached pandemic proportions.

In order to cope with the world and the society that we find ourselves living in, we build up a shield of pride and this helps us to feel acceptable - by gaining respect or a good reputation. But, society doesn't reward our achievements any further than to 'stamp out' another medal or title before moving on to the next in line. Are these rewards really worth anything at all, or do they fill a hole with something temporary? Heroes are soon forgotten as others wait to step into their 'still warm' shoes; no-one is indispensable in our society. We can find ourselves at a loss when our services are 'no longer required' - all we're left with are fading memories, and a future in which we clearly see the 'finish line' that we'll soon have to cross - 'Now Syndrome'* then takes on a whole new and less exciting meaning. Because our lives are relatively short, we've become selfish and proud - taking what we can get while we still can. Because we can't see the results of any effort to change within our lifetime, there's little motivation to change anything for the benefit of 'future' generations - as evidenced by the way we treat our world now. Our personalities are masks - personas that we're proud of and love to defend - if we see this then what's actually happening becomes clear as day. Problems occur when we don't want to strip off these masks any more than we want to walk down the street naked. If we *want* to find truth, and something new, then we must accept *unconditionally* the necessity to leave behind pride, illusions, personalities, titles, certificates and medals. I'd suggest that now - *before* we die - is a good time to begin the process.

* *Discussed in 'Sensation, Desire & Relevant Reflections'.*

Hidden

I listened to your lies of all shapes and sizes
Of colours and words in your master disguises
I never knew the centre could be
The infinite roots that you'd hidden from me

So fare thee well
And good-bye my friend
The truth must come out in the end
The clouds are dispersing
They're almost gone
And now is the time …
To sing out my song

I lived with all your fears, tears and
maddening abstractions
Like love, lust and your comical actions
I never knew the centre was free
This heartfelt love that was always in me

So fare thee well

Adieu my friend

It will all come right in the end

The lying is over

Your treachery clear

It took me a while

To breach this frontier

So fare thee well

Au revoir my friend

The truth is out - now the light won't bend

This night has passed

And it's almost day

I'm not sure where I'm going

But I'm sure on my way

A Compendium of Thoughts

*If you're following me and I'm following you
then we must be going round in circles.*

~Suffering ~

I'd suggest there isn't a 'soul' alive who can state for certain what the true nature of a human being is, how we got to be here, or what we're supposed to be doing with our lives. There's no doubt that what we're doing to our world isn't in our best interest, nor that of the wonderful creatures we share it with; everything is suffering unnecessarily in one way or another - physically and psychologically. This suffering is 'alive'; it passes between us from generation to generation, government to government, book to book and from film to film, like a mutating virus passing through the physical and metaphysical veins of humanity, and for the foreseeable future there appears to be no respite. Humanity is the cause *and* effect of its own adversity. The media is so full of the suffering going on in the world that we're becoming immune to it - so much so that it takes a horrific image, of perhaps a disaster victim, to catch our attention, but even that image can't hold it for long. We talk about suffering for a moment or two and then get on with our daily lives expecting various 'peace' organisations to get their act together and bring it to an end - turning our backs on it after our initial outcry. We feel safe and comfortable behind our walls and borders, believing that these events are nothing to do with us, *personally*.

Suffering - of humans, animals and the environment - is entertainment on our screens; we decorate our online walls with horrific images kidding ourselves that this will help to eradicate the problem. Advertising these images doesn't alleviate the problem - it serves to increase levels of fear, hatred and division. There isn't one of us who doesn't know this though with some, it's buried so deep that they can't see it. To put this into perspective; we go to war, glorify and reward the 'heroes' of that war and *then* declare horror at the images of the resulting devastation - we applaud the cause and subsequently condemn the effect. We then make films - and games - about these horrors (even re-enacting battles on their anniversaries) and they become highly profitable best sellers; as if the horror itself isn't enough, we're willing to *pay* to see more of it.

Images - of suffering are more powerful and influential than most people realise and we put them everywhere arguing that we need to be informed, yet despite being regularly 'informed' these things keep happening and we keep passively discussing them. How will the nightmare ever end if we don't take responsibility for it? We claim that the corporations, governments, army, navy and terrorists etc. are responsible, but they're human beings just like us. They're no different to you or me except that they're willing and know how to take advantage of our fear *and* we allow them to do it - one gives the order and the other obeys. Human beings commit these atrocities and that's what must stop. If we don't *want* war, then we won't have it. The process *must* and can *only* begin within each of us but when we want to make everyone *else* stop what they're doing then nothing will ever change. Who after all, would you allow to change *you*?

There's a sense of great unfairness that occurs to all of us at some point in our lives - a feeling of being cheated out of our chance to live in peace, because we were born into a world full of cruelty, horror, war, hatred, racism, violence, politics, religion and sickness. There's also a sense of limitation and a lack of control; we find that we must comply with regulations in a world where it's impossible to find justice. We're encouraged to make the most of things and accept 'that's life', by someone else's standards rather than our own. We inherited these regulations from an unhealthy society and they must be changed or in some cases, abolished. Very few people question this 'powerless to do anything about it' situation or choose to examine it further but if we do, it becomes obvious that we're not here by 'chance' and that things aren't all they seem to be. Together, we *can* live joyously, rather than accepting suffering as our only option and something we must endure to find peace - this is as preposterous as taking a lethal dose of poison in order to live. In 'Open-Mindedness' I talked about a feeling I once had about life feeling pointless, but since writing it my view has changed - life isn't pointless, only what I was doing with it.

I recently met a lady who believes that 'this life is it' and although she sincerely believes that, she's content to 'accept' the struggles of our world until she 'comes to an end' and, as is the case with most of us - quite bizarrely - we prefer that end be delayed as long as possible, which is somewhat masochistic. Surely it's wiser to ask why we're living in a 'back-to-back' horror movie world than not to question it at all. There's something absurd about an innocent baby being born into this mess with 'no way out'; in this scenario, being born can be compared to being thrown into a dungeon with no idea why and no chance of getting out again - a life sentence. No! No! No! This is *senseless* and surely invites at least a little investigation on our part. If anyone of us *were* thrown into a dungeon surely - at the very least - we'd attempt to find our way out again, rather than accept our 'fate' and give up?

~~~

A friend of mine said that this book 'won't suit everyone, especially if they don't like thinking' and I've heard similar comments many times before. It's true that many people don't like thinking; we're fatigued by the pace of life and already have enough to think about; however, what's the point in having the capacity to work things out for ourselves if we don't use it? If we don't use our ability to think - preferring to be 'entertained' - then someone else will do it for us and consequently, make our choices and take on our responsibilities. In my opinion, we each have a responsibility and obligation to act in a way that's guided by our conscience - to work with it rather than against it. For example, dropping pennies into a charity box and then walking away may salve our conscience, leaving us feeling satisfied that we've 'done our bit'. Perhaps it would be wiser to ask why these charities exist in the first place, and why we allow ourselves to do so little to eradicate the need for them; in our hearts, we know how to achieve this - all we have to do is listen to and act on this wisdom. Often we prefer to push aside and ignore our conscience but a little reflection tells us that we *have* one for a reason. Only we, as individuals, can begin to understand this when we reflect on it - to reflect on how we live our lives and why we tend to prefer what isn't good for the whole of humanity, rather than what is.

The difficulty in ending the suffering of humanity is that we must begin with ending our *own* first - as an individual. We must literally, change our mind. We don't think changing ourselves will make a difference, because it seems too simplistic an idea for such a big problem. How can changing 'me' change what's going on elsewhere in the world? Because it removes the walls and masks that separate us from it - psychologically speaking. As long as we focus on the suffering happening 'elsewhere', the whole will remain dysfunctional and we'll continue to maunder. Keeping our attention on what we can change, instead of what we can't, will make a big difference to *our* world; the mouse *can* overcome the lion, if it will just try, and each generation has the opportunity to do just that.

~ Impermanence ~

There's a sense of 'life is temporary' amongst us - it lies in our hearts and consciences. Years of pain and struggle have pushed the importance of this sense to the back of our minds; we choose to lock it away where we don't have to think about it again. That we'll die one day is too awful to contemplate, particularly as death - due to conditioning - is frequently painted as dark, morbid and terrifying - it's something sorrowful to be feared, and life, something to be held onto at any cost. Thinking about these things is considered by many people to be an act of rebellion or anarchy rather than intelligence but more than that, it's thought of as *risky* - we tend to prefer to live in fear rather than take risks. Just about everywhere we look looms a sense of impermanence, of time corroding and wearing out *everything*. No matter how robust we make them, a tower block will erode just as a straw house will, though the time taken for the process varies enormously - nothing we can do or make will last forever. Though time is abstract and an illusion, we must live by it, so surely it's prudent to use it wisely while we have the opportunity, rather than live in a way that tosses a 'heaven or hell' coin into the air hoping for a glorious outcome when we catch it again - if - *and only if* - we've behaved ourselves.

There's a big difference in the timescale of something like a pyramid crumbling and the lifetime of a human being. Because we can't relate to a human being living for thousands or millions of years, it's hard to put this into perspective. Over one, two or even three generations there's very little visible difference in the deterioration of a pyramid, making it more difficult for us to see the transitory nature of them. Historically, these constructions have been here much longer than we have and will remain long after our deaths. When one archaeologist dies, another takes over where he left off and another after him. *Still*, we continue to study and preserve death and history, as though it could save humanity from destruction. This is impossible. We're alive *now* and it would be far more intelligent to stop digging into the graves of those who died a long time ago; it's impossible to find something new in something old, or something new in something that hasn't happened yet (future). We have a dream to go into 'outer' space one day in a hope to find another world, but space exploration is also a 'relay' occupation and each of us knows that we won't be alive - or going on the trip - when 'or if' it ever becomes possible. Knowledge of this is a reminder of the nature of our impermanence and also that while we're delving into our pasts and possible futures there could be something far more important that we're supposed to be doing, realising or noticing - now.

We assign great value to our belongings and want to hold onto them for as long as possible, even if that means passing them on to our children who we hope will value them as highly as we do and subsequently, pass them on to theirs. Just like us, our ancestors lived a 'smash and grab' lifestyle, accumulating as much as they could in their own lifetimes and even trying to take their wealth with them into their next life. In a desperate attempt to live on after our deaths we try to 'immortalise' the things we've accumulated over the course of our lifetimes, but these are memories that we'd be better off losing our attachment to while we're 'living'. If we don't then we're merely passing on a legacy of the misery of the world yesterday, to the world of tomorrow. These things that we'd like to hold onto so much are the spoils of a world that has known and *still* knows great suffering - they can't be used to change it. We don't just pass on the objects to the next generation, we pass on their energy too, as discussed in 'Emotions and Energy'. Whilst we're occupied with our pasts and futures, rivers flow, waves break on the shore, eggs hatch, the wind blows and the sun 'rises' and 'sets'; what doesn't change is far more important to contemplate than what appears to.

A friend of mine once lost their mobile phone and they were very upset about it; not about the phone itself, but the deepest secrets it held about them that could now be discovered by someone else. This information will survive long after our deaths, even if we do wish to believe it's private. We're not only concerned with our pasts, we're also occupied with passwords, logins, electronic privacy, speedy up-to-date technology and fast free delivery of our purchases; these are the things that concern and control our world now, but life can't continue at this pace without self-destructing at some point - this message is very loud indeed.

It takes determination and effort to cover the ground between the starting block and the 'finish line'. There are times when our heads spin with all the confusion - this is inevitable when we set our intention to 'de-condition' our mind; we're trying to hold onto what we've got but at the same time, radically change our lives. We have to clear out that jam-packed dirty and dusty attic after many years of storing our memories up there with one vital difference; we discover that it's not just our clutter up there - it's the clutter of humanity and we've been collecting it for a *very* long time. Many can't see the point of deep thought on these subjects, and from asking quite a few people I know, the general consensus is that we'll find out what life is all about 'all in good time' and that we should enjoy it while we can. However, are we really enjoying our lives or simply opting out of anything that requires us to use our capacity to work things out for ourselves - thereby merely keeping ourselves occupied or if you will, filling the gap between what we think of as our 'births' and 'deaths'. We'll find out 'in good time' implies that we already know we'll *survive* this life, so surely it's worth a moment or two to think about what we're doing here, rather than taking our time for granted? Time is impermanent and therefore, cannot be relied on for anything other than 'running out'. Time decays, time rots and time passes by.

In summary, we think of death as something to be avoided and can go to a lot of trouble to pretend we're younger in ridiculously superficial ways; for example, wearing younger clothes or having plastic surgery. Neither of these, or any other way, will prolong our lives; they serve our vanity and attempt to cheat nature, but the clock still ticks. We don't know the difference between 'reality' and imagination - what we've come to think of as reality we continually reject in the hope that we can conquer life itself - we'll settle for nothing less. This attitude is misguided and the likely cause of many of the world's problems and more than a little arrogant for we each are, effectively, temporary residents.

~ The Journey ~

There are times in our lives when something makes us stop in our tracks and wonder where exactly we're heading, but such thoughts tend to be forgotten about as quickly as they occur and the 'moment' is overtaken by the pressures of daily life; for example, we have to cook the dinner, get the kids to bed or keep an appointment. These thoughts remain lost in the 'garage' of our minds amongst all the other clutter that we accumulate, like an old car we've been promising ourselves that we'll 'do something' about, but never quite get around to.

In the physical world, a car left standing for any length of time won't start without 'shock treatment'; for example, by having its battery charged. It needs help as it can't get going by itself. Deep thinking helps us to start our *own* 'engine' but it takes a while to get our motors running smoothly and confidently - our engines have been left standing all our lives. Just like the car, which needs to be taken on a long journey in order to fully charge its battery again, so we need to follow through with anything that comes our way after a 'what the heck' moment or perhaps a 'push' from this book. If we choose to shelve this opportunity then our battery won't charge and we'll remain 'parked'. Leave a car for long enough and it'll refuse to start altogether and could be costly to get going again, if at all. It's the same with us - the longer we wait, the more reluctant we become to embark on our journey.

Imagine sitting in the back of our cars expecting that by some miracle a driver will appear out of nowhere and take us to our various destinations such as the shops, work or the cinema. The idea is ridiculous and we wouldn't even consider it, yet we do this with our journey through life, based on the beliefs of our various authorities (our drivers) and our goal is to earn enough money to pay our bills and buy enough possessions to keep that same society going, or rather sections of it called 'Me' and 'Mine'. Ironically, every time we embark on any kind of journey, we leave everything we cherish behind anyway. Each time we leave our homes there's a chance we may never return to the belongings and people that we believe define us and are reluctant to let go of - yet our lives can end at any moment, without prior notice.

Yet we wait ... and wait ... and don't get around to thinking about the true meaning of our lives. Perhaps we're waiting for scientific 'evidence' to tell us that this 'invisible' journey really *is* important, or maybe for the arrival of an anticipated saviour. But this inaction puts the onus of our welfare - and our very existence - onto something or someone else. Meanwhile, we - humanity - believe there's enough time to discover what's 'true', but until we do it's 'business as usual'. It's quite a gamble to wait for the unknown and waiting isn't exactly an odds-on favourite, especially considering the direction we're already heading in - disaster. Only we can walk on our path and only without holding the hand of another, otherwise we're just following someone else in the hope that *they* know where *we're* going.

Once when I was driving - in the days before we had satellite navigation - I got lost after being diverted from my route. There was a car in front of me, that I'd naïvely followed since the beginning of the diversion. The driver seemed to know the area well because he wasn't glancing around, as we do when we're looking for a sign of some sort - he didn't appear to be lost. For this reason I decided to follow him - if you drive, I'm sure you can relate to this. It wasn't until he turned into a driveway several miles later that I realised my foolish mistake - more importantly, I was still lost and as it turned out, further away from my destination.

When we water ski in the wake of a power boat we can get into all sorts of difficulty after its engine stops; whereas we were 'walking on water' our skis and bodies then sink into the sea again and to use a cliché, we haven't a leg to stand on. We rely on the speed and momentum of the boat to keep us afloat and it's a lot of fun; dolphins have fun swimming in the wake of a ship, but fun is *all* it is and there's no deeper meaning to it or permanent change in the life of the dolphin. It's the same on dry land. Take for example a popular self-help book whose momentum carries it way up the best-seller charts; we may feel so lifted when we read it but that feeling is temporary. Primarily, this is because we're *reading* about how someone applied self-help to their life. It's a different matter altogether when we try to apply it to our *own* life because it doesn't account for our individual experiences - we can't walk the same path the author is treading.

'Self-help' is exactly that; we must help our-*self* and remove ourselves from the belief that we can plug into someone else's energy field and expect it to power our lives - our journey isn't theoretical *or* physical. If we were given a blank canvas, paintbrushes, paints *and* instructions by Leonardo Da Vinci, we still couldn't paint as he did. At best, we can create a *copy* of his work and however good that is, it will always be only a copy - a *fake*. Where's the value in that? We must create our *own* masterpiece. We would however, feel good about having received Leonardo's gifts and instructions. If something makes us feel good, it's prudent to find out why, because more often than not that 'good' is nothing more than what we want, rather than what we need. For many years I avoided the best advice I was given because the *best* advice is never the easiest to swallow and neither does it make us feel good; the application of good advice involves effort, sacrifice and risk - a big part of our journey. Good advice can sometimes be recognised by the force with which we reject it. There can be *no* permanent change unless we're prepared to make permanent changes - we have to want those changes, more than *anything* or *anyone* else.

Keeping our 'sights' on a target - our journey - isn't an easy task. The mind distracts us at every opportunity and it's easy to become disheartened. I used to feel frustrated when this happened and it can feel like a hopeless task to get back on track. But all we have to do is raise our bow, hold it steady and repeat this process until we're no longer distracted by 'Upgrades', 'Free Beer' or '50% off Sale' signs. Through this repetition the mind begins to lose its control and with this comes the revelation about how much control it has over us and also, a clearer understanding about our *two* voices; we built the 'wall' between them and only we can take it down again. It's a gradual process and we can't speed it up any more than we can speed up the flow of a river as it returns to its source. All we really have to do, though it's tough, is to keep our eye on the target; say 'Yes' to truth - whatever that may be and at whatever cost - and 'No' to the illusions. This is the only way to remove our conditioning unless we're one of the few 'blessed' by a rare 'Eureka' awakening experience. When we watch our mind closely we see how it loses its hold - it's worth thinking about 'who' realises this; *'Who am I?', 'Who am I?', 'Who am I?',* is our journey, and the journey is a miracle.

~ Miracles ~

The world can cater for all our needs. No-one needs to be thirsty or to go without food or shelter, yet our cities, towns and villages are full of various 'institutions' set up to provide these basic necessities for those who *do*. Our desires and their numerous divisions; greed, selfishness, competition etc., are the cause of the problems we delay solving. Dependent on a corrupt and menacing system to supply us with silly things we can well do without, we're unable to see the miracle of our world as a self-sufficient, wondrous and generous 'planet' - we take it for granted and abuse its gifts. The miracles have to be looked at, seen with increasing clarity and deeply contemplated. Then, because we change perspective, we begin to see things in an entirely different light.

Take for example the miracle of water; we fill our kettles, wash our dishes, scrub our floors and protect ourselves from getting wet with umbrellas - never noticing what a miraculous process is taking place. We can't know where water originally came from, or why there's so much of it, but we can think about the wonder. Water floats on itself when frozen, expands, crystallises, flows, reflects, cleanses, dilutes, dissolves, evaporates, quenches thirst as well as fire, falls as rain, snow, hail, sleet or dew, hangs in the air as mist or clouds, returns to its source and so much more - all without any help from us.

We're surrounded by miracles but can't see them and therefore, are unable to appreciate them. When we stay focused on the wonders of the world our lives can't help but be transformed and we see things differently - we change channel. A crumbling building looks very different to me now compared to the way I perceived it twenty years ago. The difference is nothing to do with measuring the further deterioration of the building, but in the way we observe it; for example, seeing that there exists a natural 'automatic process' that over time, returns everything to its source. I can't tell you how to do this, but you can see it for yourself if you're determined enough. That determination involves seeing the futility of the way we live now and realising that we're powerless to change anything unless we change ourselves; as I've said many times before, it's a process of negation; we must all change sooner or later - no exceptions.

A 'new born baby' is a miraculous reminder of how far from innocence we've drifted and continue to drift away from. A 'toddler', a reminder of how much we don't mind that these babies lose their innocence and how foolishly we prepare them to become 'streetwise', so that they can live *successfully* in the complicated, violent, decadent, threatening and competitive world we've created for them - rarely, if ever, to notice the miracle of their own existence. As they grow, they become mirrors of ourselves and then, because we don't approve of what we see in them, families become divided by children who complain about their parents, and parents who complain about their children. Parents compete with parents for the best dressed and equipped children - providing them with the masks and toys that society wants them to have. It's difficult to know how to break the chain and very few people have the energy to think about it; we've become disheartened and frustrated by this inherited chain of psychological disorder, because we feel powerless; however, we *are* that society and only we can change it. Each one of us in our turn was once the miraculous innocent new born baby - I'd suggest that thought is a valuable one to ponder on.

One of the greatest miracles that we ignore is the miracle of our own existence. From the joining of a sperm and an egg we become a single cell; we don't think about where the sperm or egg come from. The sperm and eggs are somehow produced by our bodies and most of them go to 'waste'; not all of a woman's eggs become part of a human being and out of *millions* of sperm cells produced by a man, only one - under the right circumstances - gets to fertilise an egg. The miraculous process of procreation has become little more than a joke and a highly profitable business; we've turned the beauty of human reproduction into an immoral multi-veined industry - advertising, porn, violence, degradation and 'a relay society' are just a few examples of these veins. Many miracles take place during the creation of a baby and continue after it's born; a baby grows, changes, learns and in due time apart from its nails and hair, stops growing. The above is highly simplistic compared to the rest that goes on in this process but my point is that we don't see or think about how the hair on our heads can grow so long, but not our eye lashes, any more than we think about where a supermarket gets its apples from. We tend to see things that our senses attract us to, but never think about the miracle of these senses or the fact that we have them in the first place. Mostly oblivious to the miracles that surround us, we continue in our acquisitive lifestyles, forgetting that without prior notice we can lose everything we value so highly in the next moment. Still, we cling to our delusional arrogance that we can conquer 'outer space', control the universe and believe that we're in control of our lives. We each have a time limit in these bodies, ordained or otherwise. There's nothing to lose in thinking about this, so why are we so afraid to do so?

~ Nothing for Nothing ~

I've written a great deal about humanity in my books and on many subjects that ultimately lead to *the* big question; 'Who am I?'. On the way to that question, many thoughts arise that challenge our existence and purpose - showing the futility of the way we live and how it leads to further suffering. One example of this is how we destroy the beautiful creatures that share our 'home' with us; elephants, tigers and other creatures we hunt down. We destroy them, and then set up institutions to protect the few that are left - if this isn't insane then I don't know what is. Apart from the excessive consumption of products and information that lead to the rapid advancement of a technological evolution and a psychological devolution, we're inactive. Each of us is one of billions, who passively observe this horror unfold and this makes us miserable as everyone 'on the stage' appears to be in control, while *we* feel powerless to change what's happening - we accept this powerlessness and at the same time, complain about it. Rather than ask the question 'Who am I?' we're more interested in who or what we can become on that 'stage'; for example, free, rich, healthier, attractive, famous or even infamous - thus adding to our problems. We enjoy applauding, criticising, comparing ourselves to and 'rating' others - one of the reasons we enjoy films, news, comedies and reality shows so much.

We seek a 'high life' - an *easy* life - not to have to work or *think* about a lack of money for the duration of our lives and we call this state 'success'; this success requires either hard work *or* 'luck', but no matter how we achieve it we must still leave it all behind one day - it's superficial. It's not because we're *innately* lazy that we look for this 'high life', but because we're weary and resentful of the treadmill that supports a system that serves no good purpose whatsoever. 'Deep down', we want 'out' of the 'rat race' - we *know* it's fruitage is poisonous; however, this is the 'highest' life that society has to offer, so we 'tread-on' hoping to achieve it knowing that there are too many applicants for the few positions available and consequently, 'slump onto our couches' in frustration. It's because of this boredom - and loneliness - that we succumb to any sensational pleasure we can find - in many ways it's our 'reward'.

No matter how much money we may accumulate to live 'higher' we'll never find happiness, contentment or more importantly, the security that we seek, because we'll *still* be all we have for company if we get 'there' - the same face looking back at us in the mirror, only much older; the same conversations going on in our head, only more bitter. There isn't any place we can be in the world or any level of 'success' we can achieve that will change how we feel about ourselves.

There are times when we may feel a surge of energy to change something, because we've had enough, like when we decide to make a stand against something in our life that has been problematic for a long time. We may, for example, write a letter of complaint to our employer about being over worked or the laziness and incompetence of our colleagues that lead to an increase in our own workload, while they take it easy. Those of us who find ourselves in this position tend to 'unwind' once we've written the letter and then spend hours editing it, until we talk ourselves out of handing it over at all. Our motives for editing the letter are many and varied; for example:

- We fear upsetting people.
- After writing our letter our anger has dissipated and we may even feel regret.
- We take the blame and convince ourselves that we're being unreasonable and making too big a deal of it.
- We're not ready to let go of the problem.
- We walk to the edge of change, but then fear the change we seek.

- We fear the unknown.
- We fear the fallout of our 'betrayal'.
- It's not team-spirited.
- We'd prefer that our employer realise what's going on for himself.

So we back off and allow resentment to build up and the problem to continue. The new version of our letter doesn't resemble the original in any way. In fact, often it ends up more like an apology for our inadequacy rather than a complaint against our colleagues; for example, 'I'm sorry, but I just can't cope with this workload'. The familiar may not be *much* but it feels secure in some perverse way nevertheless. The fact that we're doing the work of others arrives because we feel it should be done and we assume responsibility for it. We were never forced to do somebody else's work and therefore, not accountable should it not get done. The whole drama however, is *entirely* of our own making and stems from a will to change others to our way of thinking, rather than to change ourselves. Importantly, this drama is known only to ourselves; no one else is aware of our anxiety and *more* importantly, the problem remains unresolved.

~~~

It's no good acquiring thoughts from self-help books or wise men and women; this knowledge is worthless unless it's applied. I read a one star review of a random self-help book and the reviewer said 'There isn't treasure here … just the promise of it'. This reviewer was looking for answers, which are impossible to get from a book, or its author. We must do the work ourselves and know that there *is* work to be done. Imagine, if you will, holding a bottle of medicine and expecting to get better just by reading the instructions - it isn't going to happen. Similarly, whoever wrote the above review was obviously disappointed that the author's 'prescription' didn't deliver its promise. The reviewer was looking for 'quick-fix' answers outside in order to heal what was hurting on the inside - little wonder in a world of 'instant-on', 'no-effort-required' lifestyles. When the reviewer didn't get what they wanted they attacked the author. The ability to do so makes us feel empowered, but in truth, we do it because we *lack* any 'true' power of our own and in its place, accept the illusion of it. Our lives have become convenience lives - they're formulaic and organised and we're fast losing our skills in favour of the 'industrial-led' lifestyles we created. Without a cause (consumerism, for example), there can be no effect (industrialism) - without the effect, there can be no cause - a chicken and egg situation. Without changing, there can be no change - nothing for nothing.

~ Promises ~

A promise is an assurance that we *will do* what we have said and the promisee expects it to be carried out; this commitment has been greatly diluted over time and has become no more than a 'throw-in' word that we have little faith in. We make plenty of promises to ourselves and others - too often without matching intentions - and these become 'heavy' reminders on our minds, refrigerators or notice boards, because we know we're expected to keep them. A promise - regardless of who it's made to - is something we hang on our 'to-do-list' or more frequently, on our '*not*-to-do-list' - which is usually much longer. These promises tend to consist of things like sticking to a diet, drinking less, spending less money, studying more, returning something we've borrowed or doing a favour for a friend. They get pushed to one side in favour of the things we kid ourselves are more important - these tend to be our 'habits' like going shopping, doing the housework, watching television, doing the laundry or any other mundane routines we may have.

Promises get forgotten about until we meet up with the 'promisee'. We tend to feel worse than they do about the unresolved issue and the subject hovers conspicuously between us in that awkward familiar way that never gets mentioned, or 'forgotten' - it's there every time we meet up again and it won't go away until the promise is fulfilled, or we become immune to the reminders. Today's world tends to feel a responsibility to fulfil legal contracts rather than personal ones, perhaps because we fear fines or being sued more than we feel guilt or shame. Whatever the reason we tend to give promises, or handshakes, no more importance than we would a 'white lie' - not keeping our word is *very* acceptable in today's world of expediency over personal responsibility. These things matter if we want to improve our world and to find peace-of-mind - to stop the incessant chattering that haunts us day and night. The voices are there for a reason; I'd suggest that if we've had enough of the nonsense, contradiction and mischief in our world, then it's high time we started listening to them.

~ Procrastination ~

It's said that procrastination is the 'thief of time' and we don't have to think very hard to see how this is true - that 'putting off' doing things that require our attention in favour of those that don't. The truth is, that the longer we put those things off the less inclined we are to do them - often they're replaced by those 'more important things'. We feel that as long as there's a 'tomorrow' we may not have to think about should've', could've or ought've as we'll have time to do all the things we promise ourselves, but is this wise? Unfortunately time has a habit of catching up with us and when it does, all those things that once begged our attention, now *demand* it.

The possibility of existing - even in the minutest way - after this life can make it bearable; it gives us a hope of the permanence we're unable to experience in this world - a chance at 'immortality', or perhaps a hope that science will find a way to stop us aging so that we can live on. We know of this 'chance' through education, literature, spiritual teachers and films - conditioning - yet we treat what we've been taught as *truth*. A truth based on hope, fantasy and weak optimism that are born from fear - from the words and actions of a corrupt society. Even with this 'chance' at immortality, we tend to be reluctant to reflect on the purpose of our lives before our 'deaths' - we want someone else to do it for us. Who, or what, wants to survive this life is worth reflecting on, and why. That our life is temporary and driven by our ego is beyond question. The ego is *born* when we are and *dies* with us which makes it also temporary. Wherever there's a modicum of doubt about the purpose of our existence, surely the subject is worth reflecting on without referencing the past experiences and conditioning of others - continuing a cycle. After all, the problems of humanity can't be solved by referencing the past; it can serve as a 'reminder' or spark our 'curiosity' that can motivate us to find our own path - to find our own power. Instead of heeding this reminder, we look to others for guidance, reassurance or confirmation of what we already know.

We tend to use 'guides' for spiritual comfort, for a vain hope in times of need, more than anything else, but there's a danger that we become reliant on them so they're no longer guides but our leaders and we cease to think for ourselves. However, if we require this level of comfort then it follows that we have issues we lack the courage to tackle - why else would we need comforting? We seek it when we're feeling low; when we need a 'pick-me-up' or can't stand the mess we've gotten ourselves into any more - we look for someone to kiss it all better, be it a priest, guru or 'best friend'. Comfort comes after an event, therefore it's required to make us feel better about the past, but it doesn't eradicate it - it fixes the past in place together with all its pains, sorrows, beliefs and insecurities. The past is something *dead* that we want to hold onto, despite the certainty that we can't. Comfort tells us that it's okay to hold onto our baggage, as it's not our fault that we're carrying it; it denies responsibility and expects a miracle that will make everything better, with no effort on our part; I'd suggest this miracle *won't* arrive and that we must learn to leave our beliefs behind us, if we're to see the falseness of them. The past doesn't 'exist' - it's a memory, and we hold onto it and treat it as something precious as we believe it defines who we are. Sooner or later we must let go of our pasts; we *all* know this on one level or another and we know that the challenge to do so is enormous, yet we leave ourselves no 'time' to reflect on it - we procrastinate.

~ Positivity ~

There's a great deal written and said about positivity and much effort is put into promoting this phenomenon - with almost religious zeal - believing that it will solve all our problems, if we just stay positive!

Positivity however, can't last the course and though we feel great for a time whilst looking 'on the bright side', no psychological change has taken place. All we've effectively done is look the other way, while someone we'd rather not see passes us by. There's a promoted form of positivity that tells us 'if we think positive everything will be alright', but positivity isn't a cure for negativity - they go hand in hand. Thinking positive is a deliberate action of recognising and ignoring a negative situation in the hope that it will go away - very different from having a positive attitude to dealing with that same negative situation. Positivity, in itself, serves to make others comfortable around us and to distract us from truth; if we're looking in one direction, we can't see what's going on in another and more importantly, we can't see the whole. If we ask someone 'How are you?' we don't want to hear their list of problems; we want them to be positive and tell us that they're 'doing very well'. Try advising someone who's just lost a child or partner to be positive - there's no empathy or compassion in that guidance. In some cases, we want them to be positive because *we* can't cope with, or don't want to know about. their sorrow - we have enough of our own. No matter how positive they may try to feel, on a deeper level they're in terrible pain and positivity attempts to suppress that pain rather than to deal with it. Positivity and negativity are imbalances of the 'whole'. Like the volume on the radio, if it's too low we strain to hear it, and if it's too loud we cover our ears - we need the sound to be 'just right'. We also need to be able to listen without noisy or visual distractions - without any distortion.

~ In our 'Humble' Opinion ~

We want everyone to agree with our opinions,
but they're rather busy with their own.

When I was designing the cover for my first book (no longer available), I put up six different designs on a new website and asked everyone I knew to help me choose one for the final product. I already knew which of the covers I liked best but to my dismay, no-one chose it. There were no shortage of conflicting opinions and I tweaked the covers accordingly, until they no longer resembled the originals. In the end, I scrapped the lot and designed a new cover altogether. This time, I *didn't* ask for opinions and put it on the website as my definitive cover. No-one disliked it or suggested any changes and I was happy. Had I added this cover to the previous ones, it would've been subject to the same process and likely ended up following the same fate. By asking for opinions, we're 'passing the buck' onto others to make our choices for us and to approve of what we do - we care what people think. The more choices we ask others to make for us, the more confused we become by their subjective opinions - there can never be an 'outright/overall winner'. Interestingly, everyone liked the final cover, despite not having been asked for their opinion. The problem it seems is choice. When there's no choice put forward we accept the only option. This has enormous ramifications in our competitive and self-serving society - the biggest of which is that our choices are going to be made for us and our opinions formed, based on those choices.

We ask for the opinions of others but do we *really* need them? I'd suggest that we ask because we don't have confidence in ourselves or our choices and that we're looking for approval, in its many guises. Mostly however, we want other people to like us and to see things our way; we value our *own* opinions and would generally like others to value them too. Our world - particularly online - increasingly encourages 'likes' and 'dislikes' and these get us into a muddle as we become confused by the differing opinions and conflicting suggestions; it becomes impossible to satisfy everyone - or *anyone* - and that leaves us feeling frustrated and as in the above example, without a book cover. Further examples of this confusion are easily found on any forum or online video that allow reviews or comments - the same applies to books, films or other online purchases.

The world is absolutely bursting with opinions and for this reason they're often given *without* being asked for. Everything we put online is asking for the opinion of someone or other - whether we want them or not - and it *will* get them. Online is our 'showcase' and it will be criticised, both online and by those who choose *not* to air their opinions publicly. We want to be noticed, validated, appreciated and we want *this* from a world whose mind is volatile, debauched, quite mad, full of violent imagery, irresponsible and consequently, highly unstable. It's from within this world that our opinions, comments and creations are both given and received. This situation didn't begin with the internet - we've always been more than generous with our opinions - asked for or not. We give them when we look someone up and down, when we listen to gossip, when we want to agree with somebody else in order to be in their favour or - in some cases - when we want to be plain nasty.

Nowadays, we rate and review just about everything before we buy it. Often we buy products based on the experience and opinions of others, yet we've no idea who they are. We also rate and review things we *haven't* bought based on our preferences and prejudices - we have many of those. The result is a world that criticises everyone in one way or another - a world where we fear to show our 'masterpieces', in case they're negatively criticised. We fear our efforts and dreams being torn apart, which - if we look at it from another perspective - means we live in fear of our own creativity and in particular, of it being marked down by others. Reviews, likes, dislikes and ratings are different names for 'judgement by others', according to their own 'impeccable' standards. This causes chaos and further division which can - and often does - lead to anger and other negative emotions being vented online. These judgements are used as successful and easily corruptible marketing techniques; for example, companies can - and do - set up multiple accounts in order to negatively rate or review the products of their competition, whilst positively rating their own.

~~~

Dishonesty plays a large part in our opinions and *correctness* has hijacked 'diplomacy' and 'tact' - painting them in its own colours of self-importance and expediency. Apart from the obvious antagonists waiting to pounce on anyone who cares to listen to them, we don't want to 'offend' with our opinions, so we tiptoe around the truth in fear of waking it up. Dishonesty therefore, becomes acceptable - and even creditable - if it appears to be in a 'good cause' like in an 'appealing' political manifesto. However, dishonesty, can never be a good thing no matter what disguise it wears. For one thing, we're highly intelligent and generally know when someone's lying to us or being 'diplomatic' - we know a sham when we see one. We also know when *we've* lied and then things like guilt and superiority can come into play - one thing always leads to another. If we ask a friend 'Does my bum look big in these trousers' we expect them to say 'No', but the very question implies that *we* think it does. What's happening is, we're asking our friend to lie to us and generally they'll comply; the corollary of this is our bum becomes bigger than ever. The lie then demands continuity - so it goes ... on and on. People don't always lie about their opinions, but when they don't then we tend to strongly resent what we hear - this can be a great way to lose friends.

What do *you* think? Is asking for an opinion courting disaster? It depends on our intention and usually that's to hear what we want to hear, which isn't always the truth. It also depends on the intention of the person we're asking for opinions from. We'd be better off asking ourselves *why* we need someone else's opinion or why we think they may need ours, and watch - *closely* - our responses to that question. Often we look for approval, because we lack confidence in our ability to make decisions for ourselves - we look for the 'green light' (permission granted) and gratification. A gratification that tells us we're good enough, or confirms that we're *not*; yes, some of us want this confirmed too, as it lets us 'off the hook'. Our minds may sometimes be swayed by the opinions of others; we may not like those opinions but often go along with them anyway. We end up feeling frustrated by our lives because we don't live them as we want to, but rather as others think we should. As always, we can't change what's happening in the world, but we can better understand it by taking a closer look at ourselves. This is how we become empowered and grow in our ability to think for ourselves. This is how to change the belief that we need the opinions of others.

~ Hypocrisy ~

If you tell a lie for long enough, it becomes your truth.

We often betray our thoughts with our actions. Sometimes these are well intentioned - like when we don't wish to offend anyone - and sometimes not, lacking in sincerity for the sake of expediency or keeping up appearances. Take as an example a person who 'lovingly' strokes a dog, with the sole intention of getting to know its owner. He's betraying the owner of the dog by acting in one way in order to impress her, but whilst he's pretending to like the dog his thoughts tell another story altogether - perhaps by thinking about kicking the dog the minute the owner isn't looking. I've witnessed someone do this when its owner's eyes were diverted and then pretend to like the dog again. Should a relationship develop between two people in this situation - or a similar one - it won't stand much chance of being healthy. How could it when the first communication was hypocritical and therefore, dishonest?

No good can come out of any situation where we behave in one way, but act and speak against it. I'm sure that - just like me - you've had friends over for dinner or a social gathering and had a great evening, but later criticised the things they said or did *after* they'd left, despite having been in agreement with them at the time. If you haven't been in this situation, then perhaps you've spent some time in a discussion with one person and immediately telephoned a friend to tell them about it, 'You'll *never* guess what so-an-so just said', from an entirely different perspective. We're dualistic in our lifestyles, particularly when we're out to impress others. This is just another way of expressing a lack in our character that we feel obliged to make up for. We also make up for this lack in other ways, like when complaining about someone who hasn't telephoned us for a few months. We feel increasingly bitter about it and create a drama in our minds about what's really going on. What we don't see is that *we* haven't bothered to pick up the phone either, which we could easily do if we wanted to; we project our criticism and hypocrisy onto others when we don't want to examine ourselves. When we fail to live up to our *own* standards, we can never be free or complete.

There's a lot more to hypocrisy than we allow ourselves to talk about - it doesn't only arise in a 'do as I say but not as I do' situation. It's an attempt to deny our dualistic nature - a cover up. Hypocrisy, for example, is at the root of pomposity; of those who raise their noses skyward refusing to recognise that they walk on the same ground as every human being - it's delusional. It's a false sense of superiority developed in order to cover up a true sense of *inferiority*. If we have to 'think' ourselves superior, then we can't be. On the deepest level, hypocrisy is the betrayal of ourselves; it's the betrayal of our heart and we do it all the time - it's a mask.

Who am I?

At the core of the fire, lie the spoils of desire.

Every moment, every minute, everything
that we put in it
Every thought, every deed, every flower, every weed
Every muscle we expand, every blow that we withstand
Every place that we dwell, every rat that we smell

Every mask that we wear, every colour of our hair
Every film that we watch, every point that we notch
Every turn of our head, every place that we're led
Every cake that we bake, every pleasure that we take

Every need we fulfil, every blush, every chill
Every wall we defend, every tale that we bend
Every nose in the air, every time we don't care
Every scar that we leave, every ace up our sleeve

Every tear that we cry, every rule we apply
Every word that we spread, every dream in our head
Every face to the ground, every idol that we crown
Every smile, every pout, every legend that we doubt

Every truth that we taint, every sinner, every saint
Every shoulder that we chip, every stiff upper lip
Every morsel that we eat, every innocent we cheat
Every tactic we employ, everything that we destroy

Every person that we hurt, every call we avert
Everything we ignore, every tally, every score
Everything we despise, every view through our eyes
Everyone that we mock, every door that we lock

Every man we detest, every time we know best
Every bubble that we burst, every person that we curse
Every cut, every mile, every step, every trial
Every stone we have thrown, every seed we have sown

Every fear, every frown, everyone that we put down
Everything we create, every heart we vacate
Every song that we sing, every touch, every ring
Every moment, every minute, everything
that we put in it.

On Reflection

We're brilliant - often too brilliant - but we're not yet wise; we don't even *wish* to become wise. Throughout this book are many thoughts, ideas and self-reflections - none of which haven't been thought out before, and each one of them is a part of humanity studying of all things, itself. We're somehow aware of our own consciousness and able to reflect on many things about our existence and evolution - though more often than not we choose not to. We walk without thinking about how we put one leg in front of the other and eat without considering how we digest our food. We do these in much the same way as we drive our cars or use a washing machine - mechanically. Incredibly, we're able to think about how our bodies work, and our thoughts too, and the implications of that are worth pondering. As individuals, each one of us can think these things out for ourselves and find, if we're sincere, that nothing is what it appears to be.

All we really *need* to see is right in front of us when we observe our world, and what we're doing *with* and *in* it; none of it is, or can be, hidden from us if we want to discover it. As an example, we follow orders every day - orders that we don't realise we're being given because we've followed them for so long. These imperatives come in many forms such as 'Stop', 'Go', 'Give Way' and 'Keep Left' - orders we're unaware we're obeying. Other common imperatives in our daily lives are 'Open Here', 'Push', 'Pull', 'Click Here', 'Queue This Side', 'Up' and 'Down' - there are hundreds, possibly thousands more - little wonder some of us live in fear that someone will 'push the button'. We can argue - and do - that we need imperatives for things like 'organisation' or road safety but would we *really* just crash into other cars and run people over if the signs weren't there - of course not. On the contrary, we'd pay more attention to what we're doing and stop looking for instructions on how to do it. For goodness sake, even our text is predictive and corrected for us - when did we become so dependent? It's through these observations that illusions begin to fall away, and very many must. It's also through observation that our minds sharpen because they're not being used *for* us but *by* us - we begin to think for ourselves again.

This 'life' causes us so much anxiety or if you will, dread; dread of what we (as a society) created with the imminent possibility of the self-destruction of ourselves and our 'planet' or, dread of the mysterious 'void' we fear entering. We don't know what's in store for us after we die and we generally have only fables, myths, legends and history to guide us and not enough time to read all the books they're written in, let alone know if there's any truth hiding as ghosts between the lines. More often than not we don't have the energy or will to search for guidance, as it's hard to know which books are worth reading; the market is saturated with conflicting information and biased reviews of that same information. We're not keen to work things out for ourselves as we live in a world full of 'experts', instructions and reference manuals and from them we expect to find out all we need to know.

We seek gratification rather than wisdom or good advice. We're prepared to take our chances on whether or not we need to become wise, perhaps because we've as much to fear in our futures as we do the events in our pasts, or perhaps because on a deeper level we're frustrated about working so hard in this world for things we know we can't keep. In the world as we now know it - as we've always known it - there seems to be little need for wisdom. We know that no matter what we 'achieve' we must give it all up again and we don't want to - it can be felt, or seen, as 'failure' and no-one *wants* to feel that way about themselves. However, failure and success are illusions that must die when we do; still, we want so much to hold onto them, because it's what we know so well. Bearing this in mind, it's understandably difficult to 'take a chance' embarking on a 'metaphysical' journey that may *also* lead us nowhere at all; if we have to give up who we think we are and everything and everyone we know when we die, then why would we want to give it all up earlier?

Whether illusory or not, our lives begin with our births and end with our deaths. I'd suggest that we've a great deal to achieve between the limitations of these two markers. We take a chance that everything will be okay 'on the night', but this surely invests all our eggs in one basket and places a low value on our lives as individuals. It's worth remembering that this basket isn't ours 'personally' - it's society's - and any decisions we make to put our eggs into it are based on information we receive from that society. These decisions originate from the past with all its horrors and as such can never solve humanity's problems. We can't repair today's fractured society with the pieces from yesterday's fractured society - our 'spirit' has been broken. We've no enthusiasm, energy or even the will to try to pick ourselves up; we're disheartened by the wall-to-wall daily dose of humanity's insanity with no end to it in sight. We're resigned to our circumstances and need to stop and 'take stock' if we want to see change. Without self-investigation we limit our possibilities and remain reliant - for guidance - on the corrupt and mischievous system we created. Because self-investigation *exists* as an ability within each of us, it's worth reflecting on how important it is to explore it and also about in how many ways we're being diverted from our purpose, by senseless and unintelligent influences, pastimes and attractions. We have - after all - nothing to lose.

"And in the end
The love we take
Is equal to the love … we make."

Golden Slumbers
John Lennon & Paul McCartney

NOTES

NOTES

NOTES

About the Author

Renée Paule was born in London and was brought up in an orphanage, despite having two living parents. Subjected to mental and physical cruelty, the trauma she suffered left her with twelve years of almost total amnesia. Six marriages later (four official), she chose to 'take stock' and began a process of questioning everything in her world.

Her take on life changed dramatically following a profound experience revealing the connection between herself and the Universe - there's no separation. With this realisation, she no longer accepted the 'face-value' world she'd once thought of as the norm.

Renée Paule wishes to share this knowledge and show how a change of perspective can provide an alternative to the topsy-turvy world that Humanity, on the whole, accepts as an inevitable way of life.

She now lives in Ireland.

www.reneepaule.com